THE ART
OF BAKING
BREAD

*The Ultimate Guide to the Secret Recipes
of the Masters of Bread*

Claudia Giordano

Table Of Contents

INTRODUCTION

Bread is the most commonly eaten food on the planet in all of its forms. It's not just a good source of carbohydrates, but it's also lightweight and versatile, which helps to understand why it's been a part of our diet for thousands of years. Latest research indicates that humans began baking bread at least 30,000 years ago.

Ancient people had already been making gruel from water and grains, so it was only a matter of time before he began frying this mixture into a solid. In prehistoric mortar and pestle-like rocks, traces of starch (likely from the roots of cattails and ferns) were found, according to a 2010 report by the National Academy of Sciences. Before being ground into flour and mixed with water, the roots would have been peeled and dried. The paste will then be cooked on hot rocks.

RECIPES

GRINDING BREAD AND ROLLS

60 min.
normal
1786 kcal

Ingredients

For 1 Servings

- 500 g Flour (e.g. type 550)
- 300 ml Water, lukewarm
- 9 g salt
- 30 g yeast

Nutritional Values Per Serving

- Kcal 1786
- Protein 59.68 g
- Fat 5.45 g
- Carbohydrate 364.10 g

Preparation:

1. Work time about 1 hour
2. Total time about 1 hour
3. Crumble the yeast into small pieces and put them in a bowl. Add salt, water, and flour. Mix everything and knead until you get an elastic dough.
4. Cover and let it rest for 30 minutes in a warm place (about 25 degrees).
5. Knead the dough briefly with your fingertips on a flour-dusted work surface. Divide the dough in half and cut a portion into four small pieces with the dough board.
6. Now "grind" bread and sandwiches, me. H. Model them. To do this, roll the four dumplings with your hands in a circular motion on the counter until the tension is created on the surface, while the rotating motion establishes a kind of spiral at the bottom.
7. Now form a loaf of bread from the second large half of the dough and place it with the taut surface in a leavening basket or baking sheet. Cover them again in a warm place for 30 minutes.
8. After half an hour, place the bread dough on a baking sheet and cut it into rolls.

9. Preheat the oven to 220 ° and then bake the muffins for about 20 minutes and the bread for about 30 minutes at 200 ° C from top/bottom until golden brown.
10. Then cover with a cloth and let it evaporate on a wire rack.
11. Enjoy your meal!

LOW CARB BREAD

10 min.
simple
2250 kcal

Ingredients

For 1 Servings

- 300 g lowfat quark
- 8 m.-large Egg (s)
- 100 g Almond (s), or hazelnuts, ground
- 100 g Flaxseed, crushed
- 5 tbsp Wheat bran
- 2 tbsp Flour, or soy flour
- 1 pck. baking powder
- 1 teaspoon salt
- 2 tbsp Sunflower seeds
- Butter, for the mold

Nutritional Values Per Serving

- Kcal 2250
- Protein 149.00 g
- Fat 156.41 g
- Carbohydrate 62.18 g

Preparation:

1. Working time approx. 10 minutes
2. Cooking time/cooking time approx. 1 hour and 30 minutes
3. Total time approx. 1 hour and 40 minutes
4. Preheat the fan oven to 150 ° C and hold the fire on for 15 minutes before the noodles enter the range.
5. Mix the cottage cheese, eggs, and baking powder in a bowl with a hand mixer (whisk), then add the other ingredients and mix well. Pour into the greased plate (25-30 cm) and sprinkle with sunflower seeds—Bake at 90 ° C for at least 90 minutes.

6. The dough is quite runny, and the finished bread is very moist. This can be changed with more bran.
7. The finished bread should be stored in an unsealed bag in the refrigerator. It freezes well too.

ONION, CHEESE AND HAM BREAD

15 minutes.
simple
2433 kcal

Ingredients

For 1 Servings

- 500 g Flour
- 20 g yeast
- 1 teaspoon salt
- 0.35 liters Mineral water
- 100 g Cheese, spicy, grated
- 100 g Ham cubes
- 50 g roasted onions

Nutritional Values Per Serving

- Kcal 2433
- Protein 104.17 g
- Fat 47.86 g
- Carbohydrate 386.04 g

Preparation:

- Working time approx. 15 minutes
- Cooking time/cooking time approx. 50 minutes
- Total time approx. 1 hour 5 minutes
- Preheat the oven to 100 ° C.

1. Put the flour in a bowl.
2. Put the fresh yeast in a cup and add the salt. Stir until yeast is runny (yeast reacts to salt - no need to add water). Add to the flour with mineral water at room temperature and grated cheese, diced ham, and fried onions. Knead all the ingredients in a yeast dough until it separates from the edge of the bowl, and add a little flour or mineral water if you like. Allow the dough to rise in the hot oven for about 10 minutes after covering it with a cloth. Then remove the bowl and preheat the oven to 200 degrees Celsius.

3. Shape the dough into a round loaf on a floured surface and place it on a prepared baking sheet. Place in a hot oven (medium rack) and cook for 50 minutes. Then do the bump test and let it cool on a grill.

Tip: The bread can also be baked in a baking dish.

PLAIN BREAD

20 min.
simple
2125 kcal

Ingredients

<u>For 1 Servings</u>

- 500 g Flour (also half whole grain, half white)
- 350 ml water
- 1 pck. Dry yeast
- 1 tbsp sugar
- 1 teaspoon salt
- 2 tbsp oil

Nutritional Values Per Serving

- Kcal 2125
- Protein 51.49 g
- Fat 42.94 g
- Carbohydrate 374.11 g

Preparation:

Working time approx. 20 minutes
Standby time approx. 1 hour
Cooking time/cooking time approx. 50 minutes
Total time approx. 2 hours and 10 minutes

1. Mix and cover all the ingredients and let it rest twice. Knead well again and put in a greased pan (I also sprinkle the breadcrumbs on top). Let stand for another 20 minutes.
2. Brush the top with water. Then in the preheated oven for about 40-50 minutes at 220 ° C up / down.

INDIAN NAAN BREAD

- 25 min.
- Normal

Ingredients

For 1 Servings

- 500 g Flour
- 150 ml Milk, lukewarm
- 2 ½ tbsp. sugar
- 2 Tea spoons   Dry yeast
- 1 teaspoon baking powder
- 2 tbsp   Vegetable oil
- 150 ml Whole milk yogurt, lightly whipped
- 1 large Egg (s), easily beaten
- salt
- flour for rolling

Preparation

Working time approx. 25 minutes
Rest time approx. 1 hour
Cooking/baking time approx. 30 minutes
Total time approx. 1 hour 55 minutes

1. Pour the milk into a bowl, add 0.5 tablespoons of sugar and yeast. Let it sit in a warm place for about 20 minutes until the yeast has dissolved and the mixture becomes fluffy.
2. Put the flour in a large bowl, mix with 1/2 teaspoon of salt and baking powder. Add two tablespoons of sugar, dissolved yeast milk, two tablespoons of vegetable oil, lightly beaten yogurt, and lightly beaten egg. Knead all together for at least 10 minutes, or until a smooth, pliable dough emerges. Roll the dough ball in 1/4 teaspoon of oil in a tub. The bowl should be covered with cling film and set aside for 1 hour to double in size.
3. Knead the dough again, divide it into six balls of equal size and cover with a cloth.
4. Finely spread the first ball with a little flour in a drop or round shape.

5. Turn the large gas oven flame on to full power and allow a crepe pan or other large lined skillet to get very hot (you can do this without fat). Only when the pan is boiling (I use an Italian flatbread) do you add the flatbread. Fry on one side until cooked. Then flip it over briefly (be careful, the naan can quickly burn now!) And brown the other side briefly.
6. Serve hot! Excellent with any curry or sauce-based dishes.
7. The finished balls can also be wrapped in cling film and frozen very well—another 1 hour. I loosen the aluminum foil and put the balls on the stove.

PESTO BREAD WITH BASIL

25 min.
simple
1948 kcal

Ingredients

For 1 Servings

For the dough:

- 250 g flour
- 1 teaspoon salt
- 2 teaspoons of dry yeast
- 160 ml water, lukewarm

For the pesto:

- 1 bunch of basil, torn leaves, approx. 20 g
- 75 g nuts or seeds, e.g. almonds, pine nuts
- ¼ teaspoon pepper
- ½ teaspoon salt
- 2 tbsp water
- 60 ml of olive oil

Nutritional Values Per Serving

- Kcal 1948
- Protein 46.06 g
- Fat 110.55 g
- Carbohydrate 191.06 g

Preparation

Processing time about 25 minutes
Rest time about 25 minutes
Cooking/cooking time approx. 1 hour
Total time about 1 hour and 50 minutes

1. For the bread, put the flour in a bowl and add the salt on one side and the dry yeast on the other and mix gently. Pour in the lukewarm water and knead with the dough hook for about 5 minutes until a smooth dough is formed. Cover the bowl with the batter and let it rest for at least 1 hour until the batter has doubled in volume.
2. For the pesto, mix all the ingredients except the olive oil in a blender or hand mixer. With the engine running, let the oil flow and grind everything finely.
3. Cut the dough into a rectangle of approximately 45 x 30 cm. Then distribute evenly with the pesto and leave a slight free edge. Then roll it up on the long side. Using a sharp knife, cut the rolling pin in half on both sides towards the center. Twist the strands of dough and place the bread on a baking sheet lined with parchment paper.
4. Preheat the oven to 190 ° C upper and lower temperatures. Brush the bread with a little water and bake it on the preheated oven's center rack for about 25 minutes. Take out and let cool a bit.

LOW CARB BREAD WITH SUNFLOWER SEEDS

10 min.
normal
1097 kcal

Ingredients

For 1 Servings

- 50 g Sunflower seeds
- 50 g Flaxseed, crushed
- 50 g Wheat bran
- 50 g Protein powder, neutral (e.g. available in drug stores)
- 2 Egg (s), size M
- 250 g lowfat quark
- 1 teaspoon, heaped   baking powder
- 1 teaspoon salt

Nutritional Values Per Serving

- Kcal 1097
- Protein 120.35 g
- Fat 46.53 g
- Carbohydrate 46.68 g

Preparation

Processing time about 10 minutes
Rest time about 10 minutes
Cooking/cooking time about 40 minutes
Total time about 1 hour
Preheat the oven to 200 ° C.

1. Mix the dry ingredients, add the ricotta and eggs and knead a dough. Let the dough rest for 10 minutes. The flax seeds swell, and the batter becomes a little firmer.
2. Form a loaf of bread and bake for about 40 minutes. I only use parchment paper on a wire mesh.

3. Before baking, you can cut the bread a little deeper (about 1 cm) with a knife, sprinkle with sunflower seeds, and press a little if necessary. However, it is just for display.

4. The clever thing about the recipe is that it always works and is so versatile. You can also use pumpkin seeds, chopped nuts, sesame seeds, salad seed mix, etc., instead of sunflower seeds. I even baked it with 25g of pine nuts and 25g of chopped dried tomatoes. You can use almost any type of low-carb seeds or nuts.

PLAY ME THE SONG OF BREAD

10 min.
simple

Ingredients

<u>For 2 Servings</u>

- 1 Rolls, (older)
- 6 slice / n Bacon
- 8 tbsp baked beans
- 300 ml water
- 2 Onion (noun)
- 3 tbsp butter
- 1 Pickles)
- 1 teaspoon Coffee beans, (roasted)
- salt and pepper
- 1 Egg (er), (class M)
- 500 g Minced meat, (mixed)
- 3 tbsp Sunflower oil
- 2 slice / n Farmer's bread (s)
- 100 g Cheese, (Munster, snack cheese)
- 2 Tea spoons Mustard, (spicy)
- 4 tbsp Barbecue Sauce
- Iceberg lettuce

Preparation

Processing time about 10 minutes
Rest time about 20 minutes
Cooking time/cooking approx. 15 minutes
Total time about 45 minutes

1. Chopped the rolls into tiny cubes and soak them in 300 mL warm water for 20 minutes. Cook bacon until it is fluffy in a pan... Preheat the oven to 350°F and drain the liquid using absorbent material. Bring the baked beans to a boil in a large pot. In 1 tablespoon of butter, slice the onions and fry them until tender. Finely grind the coffee beans with a pinch of salt in a mortar. Slice the cucumbers that have been pickled. Remove the lettuce leaves from the stems.

2. Try squeezing the rolls thoroughly before kneading them with the egg and chopping them in a tub. Season with salt and pepper, then use moistened hands to shape four meatballs.

3. In a pan, heat the oil and cook the meatballs for 3-4 minutes on each side, seasoning with coffee salt.

4. Meanwhile, cover the slices of bread with the cheese and bake for 6-8 minutes in an oven preheated to 180 degrees.

5. Place one patty on a plate and garnish with onions, lettuce, bread slices, baked beans, pickled cucumber, and bacon. Brush with mustard and barbecue sauce and finish with the remaining meatballs.

MARINATED SALMON ON RATATOUILLE SALAD WITH ROCKET PESTO AND BREAD

60 min.
smart

Ingredients

<u>For 4 Servings</u>

- 700 g Salmon fillet (s), ready to cook
- 1 Lime (noun)
- ginger
- garlic
- Thyme and rosemary, one branch each
- 4 tbsp olive oil
- 1 m.-large Onion (noun)
- 1 toe / n garlic
- 1 small zucchini
- 2 Bell pepper (s), yellow
- 4th Tomato
- 5 tbsp olive oil
- 3 tbsp Balsamic vinegar, whiter
- 1 teaspoon mustard
- Salt and pepper, sugar
- 1 bunch arugula
- 50 ml olive oil
- 1 toe / n garlic
- 30 g Parmesan
- salt and pepper
- 1 Baguette (s)
- 1 tbsp   Pine nuts, toasted

Preparation

Working time approx. 1 hour
Total time approx. 1 hour

Divide the fish into four pieces.

1. Cut the ginger into slices, grate the lime zest, press the garlic briefly and mince the herbs.
2. Prepare a marinade with oil, lime zest, ginger, herbs, and garlic in a skillet. Soak the salmon for 6 hours, preferably covered in the refrigerator.
3. Next, spread out four aluminum foil sheets, wrap the fish in a little marinade, and grill for 6-10 minutes. Then season with salt and pepper.
4. Slice the garlic clove and use the cut side to perfume the inside of a bowl. Peel the onion and cut it into cubes. Wash and clean the vegetables, remove the seeds, and cut them into cubes. Mix everything in a bowl and let it rest.
5. Mix the vinegar, mustard, and spices in a bowl with a whisk. Now add the oil, stirring constantly. Add a pinch of sugar and marinate the salad with the vinaigrette.
6. Clean and wash the rocket and then dry it again.
7. Mix the olive oil with the peeled garlic clove, the pine nuts, and the arugula in a blender. Don't stir for long. Otherwise, the pesto will taste bitter. Now add the Parmesan and briefly puree again, seasoning with salt and pepper if necessary.
8. Bread should be cut into slices and browned on both sides of the rack. Until serving, drizzle with a little oil.
9. Service: Cover the dish with aluminum foil in its juice on the plate and, if necessary, season it with salt. Add some ratatouille salad, serve the pesto with the fish in a small bowl, or spread directly over the salmon. Season the toasts with olive oil if desired. Enjoy your meal!

GLUTEN-FREE KITCHEN MAGIC BREAD

20 min.
normal

Ingredients

<u>For 1 Servings</u>

- 350 g Flour mix (bread mix from Schär), gluten-free
- 100 g Buckwheat flour
- 50 g Flour mix (dark flour mix from Seitz), gluten-free
- 1 ½ tsp Himalayan salt or sea salt
- 50 g Flaxseed, yellow
- 50 g sesame
- 10 g Amaranth, puffed
- 2 tbsp Psyllium husks
- 1 tbsp Chia seeds
- 2 tbsp Apple Cider Vinegar
- 1 tsp, leveled sugar
- 1 cube yeast
- 550 ml Water, warm
- Something Butter for the mold

Preparation

Processing time about 20 minutes
Rest time about 15 minutes
Cooking/cooking time approx. 10 minutes and 1 hour
The total time is approximately 1 hour and 45 minutes.

Crumble the yeast and dissolve it with the sugar in the water. This takes 5 to 8 minutes. Mix last.

1. In the meantime, weigh or measure all the remaining dry ingredients, put them in a bowl, and mix. In the food processor, combine the apple cider vinegar, water, and yeast mixture and process for at least 10 minutes. T, It's also possible to do this with a hand mixer, but it's time-consuming. The dough should still be sticky but pliable; depending on the flour form, add a little more water.

2. Then butter a rectangular shape and put the dough (I divide it in half and make small loaves) in the form next to each other. Place in the oven, cover with a tea towel and set the range to a maximum temperature of 40 ° C. Let it rest for 15 minutes.

3. Remove the cloth and, with a knife, scrape the bread about four times 1 cm long. Leave to rest in the oven and set the range to 200 ° C, upper and lower temperature, and the timer to 60 minutes. The oven door must remain on during the cooking time. After 60 minutes, remove the bread from the mold and bake it for another 10 - a maximum of 15 minutes with the base facing up. Leave to cool for a few hours on a wire rack.

4. The flour mixture is essential for the taste, especially with gluten-free bread. With other flours that can be used, the taste is different. Wheat and seeds can be traded freely, eg. For example, hemp or sunflower seeds, pumpkin or walnut seeds are also possible.

BREAD AND TOMATO SALAD WITH SHEEP CHEESE

10 min.
normal
438 kcal

Ingredients

For 2 Servings

- 5 m.-large Tomatoes)
- 3 slice / n Bread (country bread)
- 80 g Sheep cheese
- 1 tbsp butter
- 1 tbsp olive oil
- 1 toe / n garlic
- 3 branch / s Oregano or 1 teaspoon dried
- 1 pinch (s) sugar
- salt
- pepper1 tbsp

Nutritional Values Per Serving

- Kcal 438
- Protein 14.14 g
- Fat 25.02 g
- Carbohydrate 37.69 g

Preparation

Working time approx. 10 minutes.
Cooking time/cooking time approx. 10 minutes
Total time approx. 20 minutes

1. Cut the bread into cubes and fry well on all sides in a pan covered with butter and set aside.
2. Wash and chop the tomatoes. Crumble the pecorino cheese or cut it into cubes. Wash and dry the oregano and remove the leaves.

3. Put the tomatoes, bread, and pecorino cheese in a bowl. Peel, squeeze, and add the garlic clove. Add the oregano, sugar, vinegar, and olive oil, mix well and season with salt and pepper.

NAAN BREAD

15 minutes.
simple
1653 kcal

Ingredients

For 1 Servings

- 250 g Flour (type 550 or spelled flour type 630)
- 1 teaspoon Dry yeast with baking powder
- Something salt
- 1 teaspoon sugar
- 100 ml Lukewarm water
- 75 g yogurt
- 2 tbsp oil
- 2 tbsp Clarified butte

Nutritional Values Per Serving

- Kcal 1653
- Protein 35.73 g
- Fat 69.64 g
- Carbohydrate 217.12 g

Preparation

Processing time about 15 minutes
Rest time about 3 hours
Cooking time/cooking approx. 8 minutes
Total time about 3 hours 23 minutes

1. Mix the flour, dry yeast with baking powder, one teaspoon of salt and sugar in a bowl. Mix the yogurt and oil, mix with the flour mixture. Pour 100 ml of warm water. Knead with the dough hook on the electric mixer until smooth.
2. Cover the dough and let it rest for 3 hours (longer if you have time) until the dough has doubled in volume. Preheat the oven to 260 degrees Celsius and prepare a baking sheet.

3. Knead the dough vigorously on a lightly floured work surface and divide it into six equal portions. Divide them one after the other into oval cakes (about 20 cm long). Put three patties on a sheet of paper. Place the flatbread on baking paper in a hot pan and bake in the oven center for 6-8 minutes until golden brown.

4. Melt the clarified butter. Place the focaccia on a rack to cool and immediately brush with a little clarified butter. Cook and brush the remaining buns in the same way. It should be served fresh.

THE LOW-CARB BREAD

10 min.
simple

Ingredients

For 1 Servings

- 200 g Oat bran
- 70 g Mixed seeds (sunflower seeds, pumpkin seeds ...)
- 50 g Sweet lupine flour or almond flour
- 50 g Flaxseed meal
- 3 tbsp Psyllium husks, approx. 25 g
- 1 pck. Tartar baking powder or regular baking powder
- 250 g lowfat quark
- 3 Egg (s)
- 1 tbsp olive oil
- 1 tbsp Balsamic vinegar or apple cider vinegar
- 1 teaspoon salt
- 2 tbsp water

Preparation

Working time approx. 10 minutes.
Cooking time/cooking time approx. 55 minutes
Total time approx. 1 hour 5 minutes

1. Mix the seeds and the different flours well with the powdered tartar. In another bowl, mix the cottage cheese with the eggs, oil, vinegar, water, and salt.
2. Now mix the quark mixture well with the flour mixture and knead it vigorously. Roll into a loaf and bake in a baking dish or baking sheet.
3. Bake the bread for 45 - 55 minutes at 180 ° C (convection oven).

DELICIOUS BREAD WITH BUTTERMILK, SPELLED AND WHEAT FLOUR

15 minutes.
Simple

Ingredients

For 4 Servings

- 250 g Buttermilk
- 250 g water
- 250 g Spelled flour (type 630)
- 300 g Wheat flour (type 405)
- 100 g oatmeal
- 4 tsp sourdough
- 1 tbsp salt
- 2 Tea spoons Sugar, possibly brown
- 1 pck. Dry yeast

Preparation

Processing time about 15 minutes
Rest time about 1 hour
Total time about 1 hour and 15 minutes

1. First, you put the buttermilk and water, flour, and all the other ingredients into the bread maker and knead well. After kneading again, the dough is placed in a breadbasket. If it is too soft, you can knead a little more flour. There I let it go again for about 15 minutes.
2. I baked the bread at about 250 ° C for about 10 minutes, then the temperature was lowered to 180 ° C, and the bread stays in the oven for about 20 minutes. To get a good crust, I poured about 150ml of water into the bottom of the range and put a bowl of water on the bottom. It's okay if it's golden brown and hollow on the bottom, just like other kinds of bread.
3. The first try with cream cheese and watercress was tasty and tastes great with cheese, jam, or whatever you want for breakfast.
4. I read dozens of recipes, looked at what was in the cupboard and the refrigerator, changed all the recipes a bit, and the result was a delicious bread.

DELFINA'S VITAL CORE BREAD

10 min.
normal
3196 kcal

Ingredients

<u>For 1 Servings</u>

- 470 g Sourdough, (rye sourdough)
- 240 g Rye flour, type 1150
- 170 g Wheat flour, type 1050
- 250 g water
- 16 g salt
- 10 g yeast
- 50 g Kernels, (vital core mix)

Nutritional Values Per Serving

- Kcal 3196
- Protein 100.42 g
- Fat 36.89 g
- Carbohydrate 608.59 g

Preparation

Processing time about 10 minutes
Rest time about 1 hour and 10 minutes
Cooking time/cooking time about 55 minutes
Total time about 2 hours and 15 minutes

1. Mix all the ingredients in the food processor with the spiral mixer on level 2 for 6 minutes. Leave covered for 10 minutes.
2. Place the dough on a floured work surface, knead again, then work in the round and then for a long time. Place in a sourdough basket, cover, and cook for about 1 hour.
3. Preheat oven to 250° O / U (preferably with a baking stone). Tilt the bread gently over the baking stone (you can slide the pencil over the bread once if you want). Push with a broad swath of your hand. Bake for 15 minutes at 350

degrees Fahrenheit, then reduce to 200 degrees Fahrenheit and bake for another 40 minutes.

4. The essential vital mix consists of: Sunflower seeds, pumpkin seeds, toasted soy, and pine nuts

BREAD FOR T-ULTRA 3 L

30 min.
normal
2146 kcal

Ingredients

For 1 Servings

- 250 g wheat flour
- 250 g Spelled flour, or of your choice
- 1 bag / n Dry yeast
- 2 tbsp oil
- 1 tbsp sugar
- 1 tbsp salt
- 350 ml Lukewarm water
- Oil, or margarine

Nutritional Values Per Serving

- Kcal 2146
- Protein 57.24 g
- Fat 45.11 g
- Carbohydrate 364.86 g

Preparation

Working time approx. 30 minutes.
Rest time approx. 2 hours.
Cooking time/cooking time approx. 40 minutes
Total time approx. 3 hours and 10 minutes

1. Put everything in a large bowl and knead until you have a dough with your hands, a dough hook, or a wooden spoon. Put the lid on and let it grow to double in size in a warm place. Place the bowl on a floured surface and knead. Grease the Ultra Bowl or rub it with margarine.
2. Preheat the oven to 190 degrees.

3. Let the bread rise in the Ultra for another 20 minutes, then bake for 40 minutes. Remove the lid, remove it from the mold, turn off the oven and leave it in the oven for another 5 minutes. Take out, wrap in a towel and let cool.

Advice: Also great for pizza toppings, fried onions, etc.

PLUM AND WALNUT BREAD

10 min.
normal
2919 kcal

Ingredients

For 1 Servings

- 375 ml Water, lukewarm
- 1 ½ tsp salt
- 300 g Wheat flour type 550
- 300 g Spelled flour
- 1 ½ pack Dry yeast
- 80 g Walnuts
- 120 g Prune (noun)
- 1 pinch (s) Bread spice mix

Nutritional Values Per Serving

- Kcal 2919
- Protein 84.90 g
- Fat 65.88 g
- Carbohydrate 481.66 g

Preparation

Working time approx. 10 minutes
Cooking time/cooking time approx. 3 hours and 30 minutes
Total time approx. 3 hours 40 minutes

1. First, pour the water and salt into the pan of the bread maker. Then add the flour with the flavors for the bread and sprinkle with the yeast. For this, I use the integral program of my bakery.
2. When the machine gives the signal to add more ingredients, add the walnuts and prunes. The ratio of walnuts to plums can vary, of course, but I prefer more plums than walnuts.
3. Each dough should be runny and not too hard. You can add a little water if it's too close. If the dough is too runny, gradually add flour when kneading.

4. When it comes to dry yeast, the best thing to do is to look at the amount of flour: one pack of my dry yeast is enough for 500g of flour, so I add 1 1/4 to 1 1/2 packets of yeast to the flour ... the recipe is based on a 1000g bread.

KNOFEL - ZWOFEL – BREAD

20 min.
simple
4756 kcal

Ingredients

<u>For 1 Servings</u>

- 1 kg Flour
- 2 large Onion (noun)
- 200 g Choice of cheese
- 2 dice yeast
- 500 ml Lukewarm water
- 3 teaspoons, cut. salt
- Fat for the shape
- Flour for the mold

Nutritional Values Per Serving

- Kcal 4756
- Protein 177.27 g
- Fat 97.46 g
- Carbohydrate 771.49 g

Preparation

Processing time of about 20 minutes.
Total time of about 20 minutes.
Scrape the onions and slice them into cubes with both the cheese first.

1. Then, in a large bowl, mix the flour with the onion, cheese, and salt. Finely sprinkle the yeast, pour warm water over it, and knead into a dough (depending on the consistency, possibly add a little more water or flour).
2. Next, form a stick, place it on a baking sheet, and let it rest for about 1 hour, or place the dough on a large or two small, greased, and floured hinged baking sheet and let it rest for approx. Of course, you can also put the dough in a regular pan or form rolls.

3. Then bake for 10 minutes at 200 ° C in a preheated oven, then lower to 180 ° C and bake for another 60 minutes until the bread has a light brown crust.
4. Attention: the cooking time depends a lot on the shape of the bread, whether it be one or more loaves or rolls. Therefore, it is better to check more frequently and reduce cooking times if necessary.
5. The bread is super simple, delicious, and tastes better with a little butter.

Tip: Of course, you can add herbs or other spices to your liking, but we like bread too.

LOW CARB BREAD - MY BEST II

15 minutes.
Normal

Ingredients

For 1 Servings

- 120 g Ground almonds
- 40 g Hemp flour
- 40 gFlax flour
- 35 g Walnut flour (walnut protein)
- 60 g Psyllium husk meal
- 40 g Pumpkin seeds or others
- 3 tbsp sesame
- 1 teaspoon salt
- 28 g Tartar baking powder
- 4 m.-large Egg (s)
- 35 ml Apple Cider Vinegar
- 300 ml Water, boiling

Preparation

Working time approx. 15 minutes
Cooking time/cooking time approx. 1 hour and 20 minutes
Total time approx. 1 hour and 35 minutes

1. Preheat oven to 180 degrees Celsius. •preheat to 350°F and prepare a baking sheet by lining it with parchment paper.
2. Put all dry ingredients in a bowl and mix well with a spoon or wooden spoon. The yeast needs to be evenly distributed. If necessary, mash something with a spoon if there are lumps or sift it first. Add eggs and vinegar. To ensure the eggs are evenly distributed, use a hand mixer with a dough hook.
3. Place the bowl on the scales, add 300 g (equivalent to 300 ml) of boiling water (possibly boiling in a kettle), and mix immediately and vigorously with the dough hook until the dough is firm everything sticks. If you mix poorly, air gaps can appear in the bread afterward.

4. Now place the dough with a scraper or carefully with your fingers (be careful, the dough can still be very hot) from the bowl onto the work surface and press or knead it. Don't be apart! The dough should be firm.
5. Now shape the space as you wish. Pulse, E.g., From the top of the dough into the dough bowl very lightly so that the holes are closed, turn the bowl over and let the dough fall. The molding is done.
6. Place the dough in the oven on the baking sheet and bake for 70 minutes without convection on the second track from the bottom. During this time, don't open the door. After 70 minutes, you can turn off the oven, turn the bread and leave it in the oven for another 5 minutes. Open the oven door, turn the bread over and leave it in the oven for another 5 minutes. Only then take it out and let it cool down on a wire rack. The bread crumbles a little, but that's normal.

The recipe makes an 800g bar.Degrees:

1. If you want to keep the bread for longer than three days, I recommend storing it in a freezer bag in the refrigerator by the second day at the latest. In any case, it should be well cooled before putting it in the fridge. For me, it can take up to 2 weeks and is delicious.
2. You can cut it with a serrated knife once it has cooled.
3. It is essential to use psyllium husks and not psyllium seeds.
4. A soft bread that is also suitable for gratins.

Tip: Toast the bread slices before enjoying them.

BREAD WITHOUT KNEADING, VINSCHGAU STYLE

10 min.
Simple

Ingredients

For 1 Servings

- 400 g Wheat flour (type 550)
- 200 g Wholemeal spelled flour
- 200 g Wholemeal rye flour
- 50 g Rye meal
- n. B. Rye meal for the work surface
- 2 Tea spoons Bread spice mix (fennel, caraway, coriander)
- 1 teaspoon Shabby clover
- 170 g Sourdough (Lievito Madre) or 50 g of rye sourdough
- 10 g Yeast, fresh
- 650 ml Water at room temperature
- 2 Tea spoons salt

Preparation

Processing time of about 10 minutes.
Rest time about 12 hours.
Cook / Cook Time approximately 2 hours 5 minutes
Total time around 14 hours and 15 minutes.

1. Dissolve yeast, sugar, and sourdough in the water. Mix the other ingredients and then add the yeast water. It works with a wooden spoon, and no mixer is needed.
2. Cover the bowl and let the dough rise for 5 to 12 hours. The travel time depends on the temperature. It should at least triple its volume and boil well. At room temperature, a travel time of 5 hours is sufficient.
3. If I have more time, in the afternoon I prepare the dough, and the next morning I bake the bread. The bowl is then in the cellar for the night. You have to test how and where the dough goes best.
4. The next day, preheat the oven, including the pot, to 200 ° C (45 minutes). Then push the dough out onto a work surface floured with rye flour, fold it once on each side towards the center, and then place it in the pan. Cover and bake

for 80 minutes at 200 ° C, then bake for another 45 minutes without a lid and let cool.

WALNUT - BANANA – BREAD

15 minutes.
normal
4456 kcal

Ingredients

For 1Servings

- 2 Banana (s), ripe
- 50 g sugar
- 250 g Flour
- 300 g Walnuts, 200 g roughly chopped, 100 g whole
- 200 g Raisins (can also be omitted)
- 2 tbsp   oil
- 3 tbsp   milk
- ½ tsp Baking soda
- ¼ tsp salt
- 2 Egg (s)

Nutritional Values Per Serving

- Kcal 4456
- Protein 98.65 g
- Fat 243.72 g
- Carbohydrate 457.57 g

Preparation

Working time approx. 15 minutes
Total time approx. 15 minutes

1. Mash the bananas with a fork or cut them into slices with a hand mixer. Add oil, sugar, milk, and eggs and mix well.
2. Mix the baking powder, flour, salt, nuts (and raisins), and mix with the banana mixture. Pour into a well-greased bread pan (30 x 11 x 8). Complete with the walnuts cut in half. Bake at 200 degrees (hot air around 190 degrees) for 40 minutes (make sure you do a boil test).

3. Instead using walnuts, you can use hazelnuts or almonds. You may also use water instead of milk.

BODENSEE THURGAU – BREAD

30 minutes.
normal
2381 kcal

Ingredients

For 1 Portions

- 100 g wheat flour, light
- 100 g of water
- 20 g sourdough mix (sour wheat)
- 100 g wheat flour, light
- 100 g of water
- 2 g yeast, up to 3 g
- 50 g spelled flakes
- 50 g of lukewarm water
- 250 g wheat flour, light
- 100 g spelled flour, light
- 50 g rye flour (wholemeal)
- 12 g of salt
- 12 g of baked malt or honey
- 180 g of buttermilk

Nutritional values per serving

- Kcal 2381
- Protein 73.94 g
- Fat 9.23 g
- Carbohydrate 484.25 g

Preparation

Processing time of about 30 minutes.
Rest time about 18 hours.
Total time around 18 hours and 30 minutes.

Natural yeast:

- 100 g of soft wheat flour
- 100 g of water
- 20 g of bitter wheat
- Mix everything and let it ripen at room temperature for 18-20 hours.

Mass:

- 100 g of soft wheat flour
- 100 g of water
- 2-3 g yeast
- Mix everything and let it ripen at room temperature for 18-20 hours.

Swollen part:

- 50 g spelled
- Flakes 50 g of water
- Pour warm water over the spelled flakes and cover overnight.

Dough:

- Wheat sourdough
- Pre-battered

- swelling
- 250 g of soft wheat flour
- 100 g light spelled flour
- 50 g of whole rye flour
- 12 g of salt
- 12 g of baked malt or honey

1. Mix about 180 g of buttermilk and knead for 8-10 minutes until a homogeneous dough is formed.
2. Knead the dough for about 30 minutes, then get a round shape with the end down. Put in a well-floured yeast basket, 80-100 min. Let it go.
3. Preheat the oven with the refractory stone to 250 degrees (upper and lower heat).
4. Pour the bread dough from the correction basket onto the baking stone (to do this, quickly remove the baking stone from the oven), push it back into the range (second loaf from the bottom), and steam vigorously.
5. After about 10 minutes (ventilation), lower the temperature to 200 degrees.
6. Cook Time 45-50
7. Minutes. It gives a very rustic look thanks to the lower end and does not cut it.
8. Wrapped in a linen towel, it stays fresh and juicy for a long time!

POTATOES - OLIVES – BREAD

15 minutes.
easy

Ingredients

For 1 Portions

- 1 kg of flour
- One tablespoon of salt
- One spoon of sugar
- Two pcs. Dry yeast
- 200 g of mashed potatoes
- One ¼ liter of warm water
- One glass of pitted green olives
- One jar of pitted black olives
- One glass of dried tomato (s)
- olive oil
- Dried aromatic herbs in Italian (oregano, thyme, basil, etc.)
- Kernel, (sesame, etc.)
- Possibly. Chilli Peppers

Preparation

Processing time of about 15 minutes.
Rest time about 10 hours.
Total time around 10 hours and 15 minutes.

1. Mix the first six ingredients with the electric mixer (dough hook). Refrigerate overnight and cover.
2. Spread the next day on a baking sheet and spread over the finely chopped olives and tomatoes (chili if desired) or press well into the dough. Brush along olive oil, sprinkle with herbs, and with seeds.
3. Bake it up to 200 degrees for 15 minutes, then at 175 degrees for another 25 minutes.
4. The perfect bread for various sauces that should not be missing at any party!

MEDITERRANEAN BREAD (ALWAYS WORKS!)

10 mins.
easy
2584 kcal

Ingredients

For 1 Servings

- 250 g flour
- 1 sachet of dry yeast
- 50 ml of olive oil
- 50 ml white wine (dry)
- 4th egg / I.
- 200 g Kat ham cut into cubes
- 100 g Gruyere (grated)
- 200 g pitted black olives

Nutritional Values Per Serving

- Kcal 2584
- Protein 127.54 g
- Fat 140.44 g
- Carbohydrate 192.99 g

Preparation

1. Working time approx. 10 minutes
2. Total time approx. 10 minutes
3. The best thing about bread is that you don't have to drop anything and it always works! It tastes best when diced with friends on a lovely evening, for example, as a snack.
4. Preheat the oven to 180 ° C and grease a baking sheet.
5. Mix the flour with the dry yeast. With the blender on, add white wine, oil, and eggs. Then briefly mix the cheese, diced ham, and olives.
6. Load the batter into the pan right away and bake for 55-60 minutes at 180° C on the middle rack.
7. Check the bread with a wooden skewer to see if it's still okay.

3 MINUTES OF BREAD

3 minutes.
easy
4026 kcal

Ingredients

For 1 Servings

- 400 g type 405 soft wheat flour
- 400 g spelled flour
- 75 g of flaxseed
- 125 g millet
- 1 tablespoon bread spice mixture (coriander, cumin, fennel)
- 1 cube of fresh brewer's yeast
- 700 ml of warm water
- 2 teaspoons of salt
- 3 tablespoons of sugar
- Fat for the shape

Nutritional values per serving

- Kcal 4026
- Protein 129.16 g
- Fat 68.37 g
- Carbohydrate 699.96 g

Preparation

Working time approx. 3 minutes
Cooking time/cooking time approx. 1 hour
Total time approx. 1 hour 3 minutes

1. Dissolve the yeast with salt and sugar in warm water. The best way to do this is with a hand mixer. Put the two types of flour, flaxseed, millet, and spices for the bread in a large bowl and mix everything a little. Any other kind of grain can be used, such as E.g ., B. Sesame, sunflower seeds, etc.
2. The yeast dissolved in water with the flour and mixed everything well. You may need to use a little more flour, but just enough to keep the dough from sticking.

Put the dough in a greased baking dish and brush with water. Sprinkle over it a little mile.Put the pan in the cold oven. Set to 190 ° C and cook on high/low heat for 60 minutes. Then immediately take the bread out of the pan and let it cool on a wire rack.

RUSSIAN BREAD CAKE

30 minutes.
normal
3389 kcal

Ingredients

For 1 Servings

- 80 grams of flour
- Three teaspoons of baking powder
- 120 g of sugar
- 1 pack of vanilla sugar
- 3 small eggs
- 100 ml oil, neutral
- 100 ml milk
- 300 g sour cream
- 150 g sweetened condensed milk
- 100 g biscuit (Russian bread)

Nutritional values per serving

- Kcal 3389
- Protein 54.90 gr
- Fat 221.25 g
- Carbohydrate 294.84 g

Preparation

Working time approx. 30 minutes
Total time approx. 30 minutes

1. Put the Russian bread in a freezer bag, seal the bag and finely crush the dough with a rolling pin.
2. Mix the flour with the baking powder. Add the breadcrumbs, sugar, and vanilla sugar. Mix well. Add eggs, oil, and milk and mix well. Put the dough in a removable tin and put it in the oven.

3. Bake at a temperature above/below 200 ° (preheated), hot air 180 °, gas level 3 for 25-30 minutes.Mix the sour cream with the condensed milk and spread over the hot sponge cake. Let the cake cool down.

BREAD CAKE

30 minutes.
easy
338 kcal

Ingredients

<u>For 2 Portions</u>

- 250 g of stale bread
- 100 goats
- 300 ml of warm milk
- 1 egg (s)
- 1 m bell peppers (or 1/2 red and 1/2 green)
- 1 large onion
- 1 clove garlic)
- salt and pepper
- chives
- Possibly. Oregano, thyme, and other spices to taste.
- a little butter or oil

Nutritional values per serving

- Kcal 338
- Protein 13.86 g
- Fat 8.96 g
- Carbohydrate 49.80 gr

Preparation

Processing time of about 30 minutes.
Total time of about 30 minutes.

1. Dip the breadcrumbs in a little warm water. Dip the oatmeal in warm milk. Squeeze the soft bread well and mix it with the oatmeal. Add the egg.
2. Chop the pepper, onion, and garlic clove, fry them briefly in a frying pan with a drizzle of oil, and stir. Season the salt and pepper, add finely chopped chives and other aromatic herbs if desired.

3. Now take some flat cakes about 7 cm wide and fry them well on both sides in butter or oil.

Tip: If the mixture is too soft, add little breadcrumbs. You can also add ham or cheese if you like. These cakes go well with a salad.

EAT THE STUPID BREAD

15 minutes.
Normal

Ingredients

- for 1 Portions
- 520 g of warm water
- ½ yeast cube or one packet of dry yeast
- 400 g of soft wheat flour type 550
- 100 g of spelled flour type 630
- 200 g of rye flour type 1150
- 50 g of quiet wheat flour type 1050
- Cut 3 tsp. Salt-
- 1 teaspoon caster sugar

Preparation

Processing time of about 15 minutes.
Rest time about 1 hour.
Cooking/cooking time approx. 1 hour
Total time about 2 hours and 15 minutes.

1. Heat the water to 37 degrees and dissolve the yeast in it. (for example, Monsieur Cuisine 3 min., level 3, 37 degrees)
2. Add all the ingredients (now add the dry yeast) and then mix them until you get a sticky dough (ex.
3. Please put it in a floured bowl and let it rest for 1 hour. Fold the dough approx. Form a loaf ten times and place it in a greased Roman pot or similar with a lid.
4. Place in a cold oven, bake at 240 ° C up / down for 50 minutes with the lid on and then for 10 minutes without the lid.
5. The Römertopf is NOT watered before cooking!

SPELLED - RYE - NATURAL YEAST - MÄUSELE BREAD

30 minutes.
Normal

Ingredients

For 1 Portions

- 250 g of natural yeast (spelled)
- 350 g fine spelled flour
- 200 g of fine rye flour
- 2 teaspoons, leveled. Salt-
- Maybe 10 grams of fresh yeast
- ½ tablespoon of oven malt
- 320 ml of warm water

Preparation

Processing time of about 30 minutes.
Rest time about 4 hours.
Cooking/cooking time approx. 35 minutes
Total time about 5 hours 5 minutes
Mix the spelled flour and rye flour.

1. Mix the yeast with a little water, salt, and baking malt. Add to the flour mixture and the sourdough yeast and knead until the dough is not too compact. Eventually, add a tablespoon of water per tablespoon.
2. Cover the dough and let it rest for 1 to 2 hours or until doubled in volume.
3. Cut the dough in half and use your palms to shape each half into a square on a lightly floured surface. The long side should be the same length as the skillet.
4. Then roll the dough on the long side and place it in the pan seam side down.
5. This will add some tension to the dough, and it will rise nicely.
6. Cover and let rise again until the batter is almost to the edge of the pan.
7. Preheat the oven to 250 degrees by circulating air. Place a fireproof container with water inside.
8. Cut the bread lengthwise with a very sharp knife about 2 cm deep.

9. Cook for 10 minutes at 250 degrees of air circulation and 30 to 35 minutes at 190 degrees of air circulation.

10. Immediately remove it from the mold and do the detonation test: if the bread sounds hollow when beating at the base, it does.

11. Otherwise, bake another 5 minutes without a pan at 190 degrees air circulation.

12. Calm it on a wire rack covered with a kitchen towel.

13. Tip 1: You can also bake bread in a large pan. However, before the second test, the batter can only fill half of the pan.

14. Tip 2: Or you can bake bread on parchment paper in the ring of a removable pan. To do this, shape the dough with the palms of your hands on a lightly floured surface and use your fingers to pull it from the edge to the center. Place the side of the seam down in the removable form.

15. With both alternatives, the cooking time is extended from 50 to 60 minutes.

FAST BREAD

20 minutes.
Normal

Ingredients

For 1 Servings

- 400 g spelled flour
- 400 g whole grain rye flour
- 700 ml warm water, approx. 37 ° C.
- 1 cube of yeast
- 1 tablespoon of salt
- 1 teaspoon of sugar
- 1 tablespoon of fruit vinegar
- 1 tablespoon of honey or oil or syrup
- North. B. Grains of your choice, up to 1 kg, including flour
- Fat for the shape

Preparation

Working time approx. 20 minutes
Cooking time/cooking time approx. 1 hour and 15 minutes
Total time approx. 1 hour and 35 minutes

1. Preheat the oven to 190 ° C upper / lower temperature. Dissolve the yeast, sugar, and salt in the water. Put flour, oat flakes, and cereals in a bowl - together approx—1000 g. Flax, oat flakes, sunflower, walnut, or pumpkin seeds taste great.
2. Now add the water with yeast, salt, sugar, vinegar, and oil and mix with the mixer. Place the dough in a well-greased baking sheet and bake for about 75 minutes at 190 ° C.
3. When the bread is cooked, immediately remove it from the mold and let it cool down.

OATS - POTATOES - BREAD

20 minutes.
normal

Ingredients

<u>For 1 Portions</u>

- 250 g potatoes, floured cooking
- 30 g fresh yeast
- 125 ml of warm water
- 350 g of wheat flour
- 100 g soft rolled oats
- 1 teaspoon salt
- Margarine for can
- 1 egg yolk to brush
- Oatmeal for sprinkling

Preparation

Processing time of about 20 minutes.
Rest time about 1 hour.
Total time about 1 hour and 20 minutes.

1. Boil the potatoes, peel them, and let cool (it can also be from the day before). Crumble the yeast in a cup and dissolve it in 1 tablespoon of warm water.
2. Put the flour with the oats in a large bowl, mix, and make a center. Spray the salt on the edge of the bowl. Pour the mixed yeast into the tub. Squeeze or mash the potatoes with a press and add them to the bowl along with the rest of the water. Knead everything together to form a dough. Form the dough into a ball, cover, and let it rest in a warm place for 40-45 minutes.
3. Pre-heat oven to 225 ° C. Grease a frying pan with margarine. Knead the dough well again and form 2 loaves of bread. Place the loaves on the baking sheet and score three times on the surface. Mix the egg yolks with a little water until the mixture is smooth, and spread the bread. Sprinkle with rolled oats and bake on the center rack for about 30 minutes. Then let the bread cool on a shelf.
4. Note: the loaves are not very big; you can also make one loaf, but then extend the cooking time.

LEMBAS - BREAD

30 minutes.
Normal

Ingredients

For 1 Portions

<u>Natural yeast:</u>

- 100 g of wheat flour, 1050
- 100 g of water
- Wheat jugs
- For the dough: (pre-dough)
- 150 g of wheat flour, 1050
- 175 g spelled flour, 630
- 75 g rye flour, 1150
- 300 g of water
- 2 g dry yeast

<u>For the dough: (main dough)</u>

- 250 g of wheat flour, 1050
- 250 g spelled flour, 630
- 25 g rye flour, 1150
- 150 g of water
- 10 g of oven malt
- 20 g of salt

PREPARATION

Processing time of about 30 minutes.
Rest time about 14 hours.
Total time around 14 hours and 30 minutes.

1. At night, prepare the sourdough and the previous dough and rest over warm heat for about 16 hours.
2. The next day, mix all the ingredients for the main dough, add the sourdough and the previous dough and knead well by hand. Don't forget to remove some of the ESG first for the next loaf.

3. Cover and let stand for 20 minutes. Then knead again into a large loaf or two small loaves and pack them into the yeast basket end up.
4. Preheat the oven to 230 ° C after about an hour.
5. And position the dough on the baking sheet, cut it up, and put it in the oven.
6. Have a good time for the first 15 minutes. Then air and bake for another 35 minutes at 180 ° C.
7. Advice: The pre-dough will be solid enough, and this is by design. It can almost be kneaded by hand.
8. There actually may be times when you need to add a little more or less flour to the main batter. It depends on the consistency of the sourdough. Depending on whether it is fluid enough or hard enough.

SPELLED BUCKWHEAT BREAD

5 minutes.
Easy

Ingredients

For12thPortions

- 400 g of whole spelled flour
- 100 g of buckwheat flour
- 2 teaspoons of salt
- Three tablespoons vinegar (fruit vinegar)
- 1 yeast cube (or dry yeast)
- 500 ml of warm water
- 1 cup / n flax or sesame seeds, sunflower seeds

Preparation

Processing time of about 5 minutes.
Total time of about 5 minutes.
This recipe comes from a lovely colleague:

1. Mix everything well in a bowl, do not let it rise. In a cold ovenproof skillet. About 220 ° 1 hour. The seeds can be changed if you wish (best to dissolve the yeast in the water first; it generally works best with fresh yeast!)

HEARTY SPELLED BREAD

20 minutes.
Normal

Ingredients

For 1 Servings

- 1 sachet of yeast (dry yeast)
- 1 pinch of sugar
- 400 ml natural yogurt
- 500 g flour (spelled flour type 630)
- 2 teaspoons of salt
- 3 tablespoons of crispy onion (s) roasted (s)
- 3 tablespoons herbs, mixed (dried or frozen)

Preparation

Working time approx. 20 minutes
Rest time approx. 1 hour
Total time approx. 1 hour and 20 minutes

1. The yeast is mixed with sugar and yogurt (room temperature). Let it rest for a moment. In the meantime, add the spelled flour, salt, fried onions, and herbs. So knead everything well. Allow dough rise in a warm place for about 1 hour. Knead the dough well again and put it in a pan. Let rise for 10 minutes.
2. In the meantime, preheat the oven to 200 ° c.
3. Brush the bread with milk and then bake for 30 minutes on the lowest wire rack.
4. The bread is straightforward to remove from the mold and has to be cooled down well before cutting.
5. Instead of fried onions, you can also think of sun-dried tomatoes or chopped olives on this bread.

RUSTIC BREAD IN THE TOASTER

20 minutes.
Easy

Ingredients

For 1 Servings

- 200 g of rye flour
- 200 g spelled flour
- 200 g wholemeal spelled flour
- 200 g soft wheat flour type 1050
- 3 teaspoons of salt
- Possibly. Herbal salt as needed
- If necessary, some bread spice mixture
- 3 awards from ascorbic acid
- 2 handfuls of sunflower seeds
- 2 handfuls of sesame seeds
- 2 handfuls of flax seeds
- ½ cube of fresh brewer's yeast (or 1 bag of dry yeast)
- 1 teaspoon honey
- 640 ml of warm water

Preparation

Working time approx. 20 minutes
Rest time approx. 15 hours
Total time approx. 15 hours and 20 minutes

1. When you are using fresh yeast, add it to the honey first.
2. Put all ingredients in a large bowl, pour water over them and mix until the dry spots are no longer visible. Cover the container with cling film and refrigerate overnight. Let it cool down for 2-3 hours the next morning so that it can rise even better. A sparkling mass has formed.
3. Put about 3 tablespoons of flour on the work surface and slide the dough over it with the help of a scraper. Now put a little flour on the dough and possibly the outside and fold the dough with your hands like an envelope.
4. Then fold just part of the center to the right and then go left and then up and down the same way. You can also mix the dough with flour (it's easier if you've

never done this before). Thanks to the flour, the dough no longer sticks to your fingers. There is no need to knead the flour; it is just on the outside and shapes the dough.

5. Place the dough with the open side down in a baking dish that must be lined with parchment paper, then cook everything together with the lid.

Cooking times in a hot oven:
7 min. At 250 ° c, with the lid closed,
35 min. At 230 ° c with the lid closed, remove the cover and dry for approx.
Cook or brown for 15 minutes at 230 ° c without a lid.

1. The bread has a beautiful crust like that of the oven. This is what the closed lid does.
2. Tips: i often use a mixture of lettuce seeds, sunflower seeds, walnuts, sesame seeds, and flax seeds. But everyone can do it as they want. It is only essential that the grill or casserole does not have a plastic part anywhere and that the size corresponds to the amount of dough. Otherwise, the bread will be a bit loose and no longer look so lovely.

WHOLE WHEAT SPELLED BREAD.

10 minutes.
Easy

Ingredients

For 1 Portions

- 300 g whole wheat flour
- 200 g spelled flour
- 500 ml of water
- 1 on / n of yeast
- 1 tablespoon of salt
- 3 tablespoons of hazelnuts
- 2 tablespoons sunflower seeds
- 2 tablespoons flax seeds
- 2 tablespoons of sesame
- 50 g rolled oats, substantial

Similarity:

Fat for the form
Possibly. Nuts for sprinkling
Possibly. Sunflower seeds for sprinkling

Preparation

Processing time of about 10 minutes.
Cooking/cooking time approx. 1 hour and 10 minutes
Total time about 1 hour and 20 minutes.

1. Mix all the ingredients with the dough hook for about 5 minutes. Then put the dough in a greased pan. I recommend grating the bread lightly in the center to have an excellent shape after baking.
2. Place in a cold oven and bake at 200 ° c from top/bottom for 60-70 minutes.
3. I also like to sprinkle walnuts or sunflower seeds on bread.
4. Hazelnuts can be substituted for walnuts or almonds, for example.

BREAD WITH SPELLED FLOUR

20 minutes.
Easy

Ingredients

For 1 Portions

- 300 g of whole spelled flour
- 200 g spelled flour
- 2 teaspoons of salt
- 1 teaspoon of sugar
- 1 package dry yeast
- North. B. Cereals (e.g., sunflower seeds, sesame, black cumin, rolled oats, flax seeds ...)
- 375 ml of sparkling mineral water
- 3 tablespoons of oil (for example, olive, rapeseed, sesame, or flax oil, ...)
- Possibly. Fat for the form
- Possibly. Brushing water

Preparation

Processing time of about 20 minutes.
Rest time about 1 hour.
Cooking/cooking time approx. 1 hour
Total time about 2 hours and 20 minutes.

1. Put the flour, salt, sugar, yeast, and possibly cereals in a bowl and mix. Add water and oil, mix and knead. Allow dough rise in a warm place. Knead again.
2. Pour batter onto parchment paper-lined or greased baking sheet. Preheat the oven to 50 ° c. Place the bread in the oven with a bowl of heat-resistant water. Then heat to 200 ° c (convection) and bake for about 1 hour.
3. If you don't like the scab, you can brush the surface with water from time to time.
4. At the end of cooking, prick with a wooden stick. If the dough doesn't stick to the bar when you remove it, the bread is done. After cooking, let the bread rest briefly and then remove it from the pan to cool.
5. The type of flour can be changed if desired.

007 BREAD

5 minutes.
Easy

Ingredients

For 1 Portions

- 100 g of natural yeast
- 500 g rye flour
- 500 g of wheat flour
- 4 teaspoons of salt
- 1 teaspoon malt
- 750 g of water
- 5 g yeast

Preparation

1. Processing time of about 5 minutes.
2. Rest time about 1 day
3. Cooking/cooking time approx. 50 minutes
4. Total time about 1 day 55 minutes
5. Mix everything until you see dry spots. Then put it covered in the basement for 24 hours.
6. Form three loaves with plenty of flour and bake for 15 minutes at 250 ° c up / down and then 35 minutes at 200 ° c. Or shape a loaf and bake for 15 minutes at 250 ° c and 45 minutes at 200 ° c.

5 MINUTES OF BREAD

5 minutes.
Easy

Ingredients

For 1 Servings

- 1 bag of brewer's yeast, fresh or dry yeast
- 450 ml of warm water
- 500g flour
- 50 g sunflower seeds
- 50 g of flaxseed
- 50 g sesame seeds
- 2 teaspoons of salt
- 1 handful of oatmeal to dust
- Fat for the shape

Preparation

Working time approx. Five minutes
Rest time approx. 15 minutes
Cooking time/cooking time approx. 1 hour
Total time approx. 1 hour and 20 minutes

1. Mix fresh yeast with water or dry yeast with flour. Add all other ingredients except oatmeal and mix well. Put the dough in a greased baking sheet, sprinkle with oatmeal, and bake.
2. Bake for about 10-15 minutes, then bake in the oven at 200 ° c high/low heat for 60 minutes (with hot air at 170 ° c for 50 minutes). Take the hot bread out of the mold and let it cool down.

Tips:

Grains can be left out or exchanged (raisins, almonds, walnuts).

The pan can also be greased and sprinkled with oatmeal before baking so that the bread loosens more easily after baking.

GLUTEN-FREE BAGUETTE BREAD

30 minutes.
Easy

Ingredients

<u>For 1 Servings</u>

- 500 g flour, a light gluten-free mixture
- 1 cube of yeast
- 300 ml of milk
- 50 g margarine
- 1 egg (s)
- 1 teaspoon of sugar
- 1 teaspoon of salt
- 50 g bacon, diced, lean or:
- 100 g grated cheese or:
- 6 teaspoons wild garlic paste or:
- Tomatoes, olives, feta cheese, mixed
- 50 ml of olive oil
- 1 tablespoon of italian herbal salt for brushing

Preparation

Working time approx. 30 minutes
Rest time approx. 30 minutes
Cooking time/cooking time approx. 20 minutes
Total time approx. 1 hour and 20 minutes

1. Put the flour in a bowl.
2. Heat milk and dissolve the yeast with the sugar.
3. Add the milk yeast with butter, egg, and salt to the flour and mix everything well.
4. Line a baking sheet with parchment paper.
5. Take the dough out of the bowl and knead once. Add some flour to keep it from sticking too much. Now cut the dough in half and press each half into an oval. Add a little flour to prevent the dough from sticking.

6. Now cover it as you like, for example, with grated cheese or diced bacon. It is also delicious if one of the loaves is covered with ram paste. But make sure that one edge runs out of dough. Otherwise, everything will swell up.

7. If you want, you can also sprinkle a mixture of tomatoes, olives, and feta cheese on top. Peel, quarter and core the tomato, then pat dry with kitchen paper and cut into cubes. Instead of olives, you can also take diced bacon and then mix everything and place it in the oval.

8. When the filling is ready, just carefully roll it up and place the seam on a baking sheet lined with parchment paper. Now pull it carefully. Cover loaves and let them rest for at least 30 minutes.

9. Then brush the bread with the beaten egg for the cheese filling and sprinkle with the grated cheese, which is now cut several times. Brush the tomato and wild garlic bread with oil and cut into slices. Also, cut the bread with bacon.

10. Position in the oven preheated to 200 degrees.

11. Bake for 20 minutes.

12. The amount of pasta is enough for two baguettes.

WRH – BREAD

10 mins.
Easy

Ingredients

<u>For 1 Servings</u>

- 300 g of wheat flour
- 200 g of rye flour
- 50 g of oat pulp
- 1 tablespoon. Salt-
- 1 tablespoon. Spice mix for bread
- ½ cube of fresh yeast (or 1 point of dry yeast)
- 370 ml of warm water
- Oatmeal for dusting

Preparation

Working time approx. 10 minutes
Rest time approx. 2 hours and 20 minutes
Cooking time/cooking time approx. 55 minutes
Total time approx. 3 hours and 25 minutes

1. Mix all the ingredients (dissolve the fresh yeast in the water) and knead until the dough comes off the base. Cover and allow to rest for about 2 hours, then knead, shape a loaf or roll, place on the pan, and let rest for another 20 minutes.
2. Make several cross-sections on the surface, brush with a little water and sprinkle with oatmeal.
3. Bake for 10 minutes at 220 °, pour a glass of water into the tube, and then bake for another 45 minutes at 200 °.

BRUNO THE BREAD

30 minutes.
Easy

Ingredients

For 1 Portions

- 5 tablespoons of natural yeast
- 200 g rye flour
- 500 g of wheat flour
- 1 tablespoon of salt
- ½ liter of warm water
- 2 pcs. Dry yeast
- Sunflower seeds or diced ham, cheese, flax seeds, pumpkin seeds, caraway seeds or
- Onion (s), dried

Preparation

Processing time of about 30 minutes.
Rest time about 1 hour.
Total time about 1 hour and 30 minutes.

1. You need a sourdough recipe; first, there are some in the database (with five tablespoons sourdough, 300g rye flour, ½l warm water, you can restore sourdough if it runs out, then it can be stored in the refrigerator for 14 days).
2. Now, prepare the dough: take five tablespoons of natural yeast and add 200 g of rye flour, 500 g of wheat flour, and a heaping tablespoon of salt. Then add ½ l of warm water and 2 sachets of dry yeast to these ingredients. Optionally, you can now add diced ham, cheese, flax seeds, sunflower seeds, pumpkin seeds, cumin seeds, or dried onions.
3. It is necessary to mix all the ingredients well and then knead the dough well. It should come off quickly from the bowl. Let stand for 1 hour. Then give the dough the desired shape, on bread or muffin, preferably with very wet hands. Otherwise, the dough will no longer slip out of your hand.
4. Then the bread is baked in the oven for 75 minutes at 175 degrees (convection). Not much for sandwiches, of course; i usually keep them in the range for about 20-25 minutes.

5. Brush with water after cooking to form a crust. It is something straightforward and tasty.

IN THE BEER BREAD

30 minutes.
Easy

Ingredients

For Six Portions

- 360 g flour (whole wheat flour)
- 1 teaspoon baking powder
- 1 teaspoon salt
- Teaspoon baking powder
- 2 tablespoons of honey
- 375 ml of beer
- Melted butter

Preparation

Processing time of about 30 minutes.
Total time of about 30 minutes.

1. Turn the oven to 190 degrees celsius. Using butter, grease a cake pan (10cm x 20cm).
2. Combine the dry ingredients in a mixing dish. There's even the butter. Pour in the beer and give it a good swirl. Don't overmix, however. The dough may also have some lumps in it.
3. Put it in the pan.
4. You bake it for about 30-40 minutes or until the crust is lightly golden. And remove from the oven and raise the temperature to 220 ° c.
5. Place the bread on a baking sheet and brush the top and sides with melted butter—cook for 5 to 10 minutes.

FRIED ONIONS - BUTTERMILK – BREAD

15 minutes.
Easy

Ingredients

For 1 Portions

- 500 g of flour
- 500 ml of buttermilk
- 1 can of onion (s) (fried onions)
- 1 yeast in cubes
- 1 teaspoon of sugar
- 1 teaspoon salt

Reparation

1. Processing time of about 15 minutes.
2. Total time of about 15 minutes.
3. Put the fresh yeast, a teaspoon of salt, and a teaspoon of sugar in a small bowl with a lid and stir to dissolve.
4. Mix the flour, fried onion, and buttermilk. When the yeast is liquid, add and mix until a compact dough forms.
5. Bring everything to the desired shape and preheat the oven to 180 ° c. We put the bread in the oven with a small bowl of water and bake for 60 minutes.

FAST LEAVENED SPELLED BREAD.

30 minutes.
Normal

Ingredients

<u>For 2 Servings</u>

- 800 g finely ground spelled flour
- 300 g finely ground soft wheat flour
- 100 g buckwheat flour, finely ground
- 4 teaspoons of salt (approx. 30-40 g)
- 1 liter of warm water
- 5 tablespoons of fruit vinegar
- 1 cube of yeast (or the corresponding dry yeast)
- 160 g walnuts
- 160 g sunflower seeds (possibly for garnish)

Preparation

Working time approx. 30 minutes
Total time approx. 30 minutes

1. Dissolve the yeast in warm water and add the vinegar. Gradually add the flour mixed with the salt, the walnut kernels mashed with the palm of your hand, and the sunflower kernels, mix well with the dough hook, and work the dough well.
2. Pour the mixture into 2 well-greased bread pans and smooth the surface with a damp spatula. Optionally, you can put a sunflower seed pattern on the surface. Cover the dough and let it rest for about 30 minutes.
3. Bake in a preheated oven at 220 degrees for about 45 minutes. The cooking time always depends on the particular oven.

SWABIAN NET (BREAD)

35 min.
Normal
2823 kcal

Ingredients

For 1 Portions

- 10 g yeast
- 75 g of natural yeast
- 520 ml cold water
- 1 teaspoon of honey
- 400 g of soft wheat flour type 405
- 200 g of quiet wheat flour type 1050
- 150 g of rye flour type 1150
- 15 g of salt

Nutritional values per serving

- Kcal 2823
- Protein 79.55 g
- Fat 9.20 g
- Carbohydrate 590.35 g
- Screen

Preparation

Processing time of about 35 minutes.
The rest time of about 12 hours and 20 minutes.
Cooking/cooking time approx. 50 minutes
Total time around 13 hours and 45 minutes.
Dissolve yeast and sourdough in a little water.

1. Add the flour, rye flour, salt, and honey and mix for 7 minutes until you get a homogeneous dough.
2. Water is given as the maximum amount. I would add 350-400 ml first (depending on the sourdough composition) and then pour more (max 520 ml) until the dough is very sticky after mixing for 6 minutes. It should be a "sticky lump" to be moist enough and retain its round shape when baking and not get too wet like a flat cake.
3. Let the dough rise for 20 minutes, then fold the dough in half from the bowl's sides. Let stand for 20 minutes. Repeat the fold two more times. Make the dough soft and sticky (with 520 ml of water, the dough sticks well).

Alternative:

1. 2 to 3 times in the steamer (automatic-> special-> let the yeast rise (20min))
2. fold back from the edge after each operation
3. Let the dough rise overnight at cool room temperature (at 15 ° c - 16 ° c, for example, in the basement, cellar).
4. The dough should be folded (it takes 8-12 hours depending on room temperature). Optionally, the dough can be refrigerated for up to 24 hours. (though hotter is faster, this step should not be rushed to achieve a more digestible result.)
5. The next day, heat the oven with a pan to 250 ° c.
6. Dampen a small 2-liter (metal) bowl well. Some water may remain on the ground. Using a damp spatula or wet hands, scoop the dough into the bowl and fold the dough in half again from the bowl's sides to create some tension.
7. Flip the bread from the bowl directly onto the hot skillet. Cook for a
8. A total of 40 to 55 minutes at 240 ° c. After 25 to 20 minutes, reduce to 220 ° c. (if you don't have a weather cooker, put a heat-resistant container and 4-5 ice cubes in the oven.)

Alternative:

1. humidity plus (heating) 240 ° c; 2-3 jets of steam;
2. 1st steam jet after insertion, 2nd steam jet after 10 minutes, 3rd steam jet 5 minutes before removal.
3. Brush the bread with water 10 minutes before the end of baking to obtain a shiny crust. Once the bread comes out of the oven, you can immediately clean it again with a damp brush and water.
4. Observations: A long cooking time (at 15 ° c or in the fridge) and the sourdough make this bread smell good. The sourdough is put on the unlined bread and does not produce growth but a delicious taste. You can bake bread without sourdough, but you have to make small compromises in terms of taste. (i use the sourdough that i bought - you can make it yourself, and you can find several recipes here.)
5. The maximum amount is given by the amount of water in the dough. Fewer water results in a smooth dough that is still manageable for advanced beginners. However, an ankle can form during cooking; h. The dough cracks slightly on one side. But this is a purely visual error. With 560 ml of water, the handling becomes more complex, as the dough sticks more strongly and flows evenly, but the bread it contains acquires its typical round shape. The shape does not change the taste; great with both variants! The crust of this bread

becomes thin and crisp and opens well when cooled. The crumb is soft and of medium-fine porosity. The inside is nice and juicy, and you can feel it crispy on the outside.

6. Bread is best stored unpackaged (standing on the cut side) for up to 3 days.

PUMPKIN MARES/BREAD

30 minutes.
Normal

Ingredients

<u>For 2 Servings</u>

- 3 cubes of yeast
- 2 kg of flour
- 250 grams of sugar
- 250 g of liquid butter
- 1 pinch of salt
- 1 liter of pumpkin pulp, pureed
- Milk

Preparation

Working time approx. 30 minutes
Rest time approx. 1 hour
Total time approx. 1 hour and 30 minutes

1. Inside a big mixing bowl, combine the flour and sugar and poke a hole in the middle. Four tablespoons of hot milk, two teaspoons of sugar, and crumbled yeast are added. Mix the baking powder, sugar, and warm milk carefully. Let everything rest for about 20 minutes in a warm place. To do this, i take a large bowl with a lid and put it in a hot water bath. When the lid is lifted, the batter is good.
2. Then add the melted butter, a pinch of salt, and the pumpkin. I cooked the pumpkin in a pressure cooker with some water until it was soft, then mixed it. Mix everything well; add a little milk if necessary. Then let everything rise again in the closed bowl in a water bath. Besides, of course, until the lid is opened.
3. The dough is enough for two large loaves of bread, which at about 175 degrees for about 45 minutes. I have five loaves of bread with approx—800 g of pasta each (175 degrees hot air, approx. 30 minutes).

Tip: freeze the prepared pumpkin so that you cannot merely bake bread pumpkins/mares for halloween.

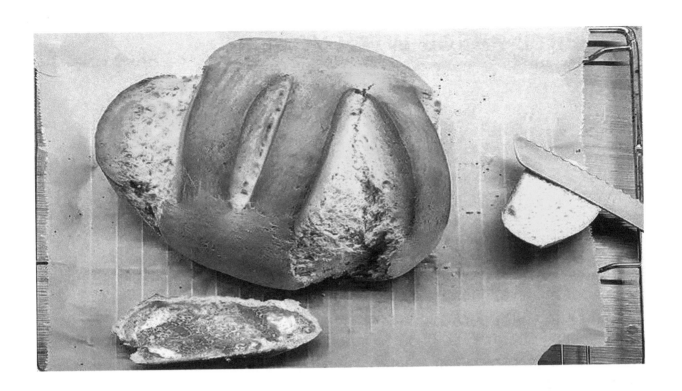

GLUTEN-FREE BREAD WITH YOGURT

20 minutes.
Normal

Ingredients

For 1 Servings

- 120 g buckwheat flour
- 250 g flour mixture, gluten-free, light, from seitz
- 120 g flour mixture, gluten-free, dark, from seitz
- 2 tablespoons of grape seed flour
- 150 g bowls of cereal, mix (hemp, sunflower seeds, flax seeds, amaranth, sesame seeds)
- 1 ½ tbs of psyllium husks
- 1 ½ tsp himalayan salt or sea salt
- 1 cube of yeast
- 1 teaspoon of sugar
- 470 ml of warm water
- 5 heaping tablespoons of yogurt, 1.5%
- 2 tablespoons of apple cider vinegar
- Butter for the mold

Preparation

Working time approx. 20 minutes
Rest time approx. 15 minutes
Cooking time/cooking time approx. 1 hour and 15 minutes
Total time approx. 1 hour and 50 minutes

1. Crumble the yeast and sprinkle it with sugar. After 1 minute, add 100 ml of warm water. After about 3 minutes, add the remaining water and mix. In the meantime, mix all the dry ingredients in a bowl. Pour the yogurt-apple cider vinegar on the flour mixture, add the yeast water mixture and mix with the food processor for about 15 minutes.
2. Brush a bread pan generously with butter. Pour in the dough, it's very sticky, but it should be. The oven's mold set the range to a maximum temperature of 40 ° c. Moisten a clean cloth with warm water and place it on the plate. Let the dough rise for 15 minutes. Then remove the fabric and cut the dough several

times diagonally with a sharp knife about 2 cm deep. Close oven door and set the oven to 200 ° c without convection—bake for 60 minutes. Take the bread out of the pan and immediately place it back in the oven from bottom to top for 10-15 minutes. (the stove can be switched off in the last 5 minutes).

3. Let the bread cool well on a wire rack. From the second day onwards, pack it in a bag or put it in the bread box.

MULTIGRAIN BREAD

20 minutes.
Normal

Ingredients

For 1 Portions

- 400 g natural yeast, whole rye
- 200 g spelled flour (wholemeal)
- 90 g of buckwheat flour (whole)
- 30 g millet, whole
- 30 g whole quinoa
- 30 g of flakes (5 cereal flakes)
- 30 g of pumpkin seeds
- 30 g of sunflower seeds
- 30 g of flax seeds
- 30 g of sesame seeds
- 12g sea salt
- 10 g of beet greens
- 200 g of warm water (approx.)
- 10 g fresh yeast, optional (*)
- 3 tablespoons of seeds - sesame mixture, sunflower seeds, flax seeds, pumpkin seeds, and 5-grain flakes)

Preparation

Processing time of about 20 minutes.
The rest time of about 3 hours.
Cooking/cooking time approx. 1 hour
Total time around 4 hours and 20 minutes.

1. Mix all the ingredients except the seeds, sprinkled with a homogeneous mixture (food processor, about 7-10 minutes).
2. Cover the dough, let it rest in a warm place for 30 minutes, then re-knead briefly (2-3 minutes).
3. Sprinkle the bba shape or a baking sheet with half of the seeds to be sprinkled. Pour the batter and smooth it out. Then sprinkle with the remaining seeds. Let

the bread rise again in a warm place (1-3 hours, depending on the sourdough's strength and the addition of yeast).

4. Bake:
5. Bba: bake bread for 1 hour with the "bake only" program.
6. Oven: bake the bread for about 50-60 minutes at about 200 ° c. (as i always bake bread in the bba, the baking information is just a guide).
7. Then let the bread cool on a wire rack and rest in the bread box for a day before cutting.
8. The quantities indicated are sufficient for a loaf of approximately 1000 g.

(*) as i have a very strong sourdough, i always bake bread without additional yeast.

LOW CARB BREAD

10 minutes.
Easy

Ingredients

<u>For 1 Portions</u>

- 250 goats
- 250 g of sunflower seeds
- 150 g of flax seeds
- 80 g flaked almonds
- Four tablespoons chia seeds heaped
- Eight heaping tablespoons of psyllium husks
- 2 teaspoons of salt
- 1 tablespoon of honey
- 750 ml of water

Preparation

Processing time of about 10 minutes.
The rest time of approximately 1 hour and 30 minutes.
Cooking/cooking time approx. 1 hour
Total time around 2 hours and 40 minutes.

1. Mix the dry ingredients well, and only then add the water and honey. Mix everything and let it rest for 1 - 2 hours.
2. Preheat oven to 180 ° c (top/bottom heat). Then put the dough in a baking dish and bake for 20 minutes.
3. Remove the bread from the pan and bake for another 40 minutes. Let cool in the oven.
4. The bread lasts for several days. I like to put the slices back in the toaster before i eat them. It tastes like freshly baked.
5. Since the cadmium content in flaxseed is relatively high, the federal center for nutrition recommends consuming no more than 20g of flaxseed per day. The daily consumption of bread should be divided accordingly.

HEARTY WHOLE WHEAT QUARK BREAD

15 minutes.
Normal
2469 kcal

Ingredients

For 1 Portions

- 500 g whole wheat flour
- 500 g low-fat quark
- 2 eggs)
- 2 pcs. Baking powder
- 1 teaspoon salt
- 1 teaspoon of sugar or honey
- 100 g of mixed cereals (for example, flax seeds, sunflower seeds, chopped walnuts)

Nutritional values per serving

- Kcal 2469
- Protein 152.90 g
- Fat 27.07 g
- Carbohydrate 392.36 g

Preparation

Processing time of about 15 minutes.
Cooking/cooking time approx. 1 hour
Total time about 1 hour and 15 minutes.

1. Put all the ingredients in a bowl and knead until you get a dough. If the dough is still sticky, add a little flour.
2. Roll the dough into a loaf and place it in a greased skillet. Cut the surface several times lengthwise.
3. The oven's bread was preheated to about 170 degrees (convection) for 45 to 60 minutes. The time depends on the oven. It is best to use a wooden stick to check if the bread is baked. Let the bread cool slightly and remove it from the mold.

4. The bread tastes good with both sweet and savory toppings.

Advice:

You can use any flour as flour, even mixed (also works with "normal" wheat flour). It, too, tastes good with blueberries as a sweet variant.

BACON ONION BREAD

30 minutes.
Easy

Ingredients

For 1 Servings

- 400 g of flour
- ½ pack of dry yeast
- 1 teaspoon of salt
- ½ teaspoon marjoram
- A little pepper
- A little paprika powder
- 250 ml of water
- 1 small onion
- Bacon cut into cubes

Preparation

Working time approx. 30 minutes
Rest time approx. 1 hour
Total time approx. 1 hour and 30 minutes

1. Dice the onion and grill with the bacon in a little clarified butter, allow cooling slightly.
2. Make a sourdough with flour, yeast, spices, and water, knead the bacon and the onion cubes underneath and let it rest for about 1 hour.
3. Place the dough on a baking sheet or baking sheet and sprinkle with a little water.
4. At 200 ° c approx. 50 minutes

MILWAUKEE – BREAD

30 minutes.
Easy

Ingredients

For 2 Servings

- 2 sachets of yeast (dry yeast)
- 200 g of melted cheese
- 2 tablespoons of sugar
- 1 teaspoon of salt
- 600 grams of flour

To fill:

- 100 g butter or margarine
- 1 bag / n soup (onion soup)

Preparation

Working time approx. 30 minutes
Rest time approx. 1 hour
Total time approx. 1 hour and 30 minutes

1. Mix the yeast with 250 ml of warm water, the cheese, the sugar, and the salt with the hand mixer. Then insert the dough hook and add the flour. Knead the dough until it comes out of the rim of the bowl. Cover and let rest in a warm place for 30 minutes.
2. Mix the soft fat and powdered onion soup thoroughly. Divide the dough into a rectangle of approx. 50x30 cm. Brush the butter with the onion soup and roll up from the narrowest part. Cover the pan with parchment paper. Cut the rolling pin lengthways and place both halves on the baking sheet with the cut surface facing up. Let rest for another 20 minutes.
3. Pre-heat oven to 200 degrees and bake the bread for about 25 minutes.
4. Serve hot or cold with herb butter or simply with soup. Bread is easy to freeze and bake again.

LOAF

30 minutes.
Normal
3388 kcal

Ingredients

For 1 Servings

- 150 g rye flour type 1370
- 350 g type 550 soft wheat flour
- 500 g soft wheat flour type 1050 or 1200
- 800 g of water
- 10 g fresh brewer's yeast
- 20 g of salt

Nutritional values per serving

- Kcal 3388
- Protein 94.63 g
- Fat 10.17 g
- Carbohydrate 709.31 g

Preparation

Working time approx. 30 minutes
Rest time approx. 4 hours
Total time approx. 4 hours and 30 minutes

1. Mix the flour.
2. Mix 200 g of water with the yeast and a little flour to make a pre-batter and let it steep for 2 hours.
3. Process the previous dough with all the other ingredients until a smooth dough is formed and ferment for 1.5 hours. Beat the dough every 30 minutes.
4. Preheat the oven to 240 degrees.
5. After the fermentation time, divide the dough into two equal parts and roll lightly with the flour. Arrange the loaves on a baking sheet and bake them in the hot oven. Bake for 10 minutes at 240 ° c, lower the stove to 200 °, and bake the bread for another 50 minutes.

VIENNESE BREAD

40 min.
Normal
2872 kcal

Ingredients

<u>For 1 Portions</u>

- 750 g of soft wheat flour type 550
- 3 teaspoons of salt
- ½ yeast cube or 1 packet of dry yeast
- ¼ liter of warm water
- 200 ml of warm milk
- Flour for kneading

Nutritional values per serving

- Kcal 2872
- Protein 91.45 g
- Fat 15.14 g
- Carbohydrate 575.95 g

Preparation

Processing time of about 40 minutes.
Rest time about 1 hour.
Total time about 1 hour and 40 minutes.

1. Sift the flour with the salt into a large bowl, crumble or sprinkle with yeast and mix with the flour. Knead the water and milk into the flour mixture until the dough comes out of the bowl.
2. Roll into a ball and knead well on a floured work surface (food processor works, too) until the dough is no longer sticky but is firm and pliable and shows bubbles.
3. Place the dough ball in the bowl dusted with flour on the bottom, slide a plastic bag over it, and leave it at room temperature for about 45 minutes until doubled in size.

4. Knead the dough again, place it on a baking tray lined with parchment paper, cover with a cloth and let it rest for another 30 minutes. Brush with warm water, cut several times diagonally with a sharp knife or scissors.

5. Preheat oven to 250 ° c. Place a baking dish filled with boiling water in the oven. Bake on the second slider from the bottom: 10 minutes at 250 ° c (hot air: 200 ° c), then 35 minutes at 200 ° c (hot air 160 ° c).

6. It is also possible to use the dough to form rolls (about 50 g in weight). Place these 2 inches apart on a parchment-lined baking sheet and flatten slightly. Cover with a cloth and leave to act for about 20 minutes. Bake at 200 ° c (hot air: 160 ° c) for 20 minutes on the second slide bar from the top.

TURKISH BREAD

20 minutes.
Easy

Ingredients

<u>For 12 Portions</u>

- 25 g yeast
- 3 dl of warm water
- 1 spoon of sugar
- 1 teaspoon salt
- 3 oil tablespoons
- 2 eggs)
- 500 g of flour
- 1 dl of yogurt
- 1 teaspoon oregano
- 100 g of grated cheese

Preparation

Processing time of about 20 minutes.
Rest time about 1 hour.
Cooking/cooking time approx. 15 minutes
Total time around 1 hour and 35 minutes.

1. Dissolve the yeast in the water. Mix the sugar, salt, two tablespoons of oil, and the egg and mix well. Add the flour little by little and knead well until it stops sticking. Cover with a damp cloth and let it rest for an hour.
2. Pre-heat oven to 200 ° c while you make the yogurt sauce. Mix the egg, yogurt, and one tablespoon of oil and season with oregano.
3. Divide the dough into 12 portions and shape it into very flat rolls (thinner than a finger). Spread with the yogurt mixture and sprinkle with cheese.
4. Bake on the top rack for about 12-15 minutes.

DELICIOUS - DELICIOUS – BREAD

20 minutes.
Normal
3520 kcal

Ingredients

<u>For 1 Portions</u>

- 650 g flour (soft wheat flour type 405)
- 350 g flour (1050 type soft wheat flour, dark)
- 1 yeast in cubes
- 1 tablespoon of salt
- 650 ml of warm water

Nutritional values per serving

- Kcal 3520
- Protein 112.95 g
- Fat 10.63 g
- Carbohydrate 722.44 g

Preparation

Processing time of about 20 minutes.
Rest time about 1 hour.
Total time about 1 hour and 20 minutes.

1. Mix the two types of flour, dig a well and crumble the yeast. Sprinkle the salt around the edge. Pour about 500 ml of warm water over the yeast in the tub, mix and knead vigorously. Add the rest of the water little by little. The dough should not stick (otherwise, there will be too much water, but you can level it with a bit of flour)—dough in my food processor. Let the dough rise for about 1 hour.
2. Then shape it into bread on a floured cloth—preheat the oven to 225 ° c. When the oven is hot, place the bread on a baking sheet lined with parchment paper. Bake for 30 minutes at 225 ° c, then another 30 minutes at 175 ° c.
3. Delicious is the bread with nutella still warm.

LOW-CARB BREAD

15 minutes.
Easy

Ingredients

<u>For 1 Servings</u>

- 500 g of low-fat quark
- Egg (s) size l.
- 1 sachet of baking powder
- 4 tablespoons of sunflower seeds
- 4 tablespoons of flaxseed, even divided
- 100 g of oat bran
- 100 g spelled bran
- 100 g almonds, ground
- 4 tablespoons of spelled flour

Preparation

Working time approx. 15 minutes
Rest time approx. 1 hour
Cooking time/cooking time approx. 45 minutes
Total time approx. 2 hours

1. Mix the quark, eggs, and salt with the hand mixer. Gradually add the remaining ingredients. Let the mixture sit for about an hour. Then preheat the oven to 170 degrees.
2. Line a removable pan with parchment paper and add the long-haired batter. The consistency of the dough is too soft to be shaped, but it is also not runny.
3. Bake inside the middle of the oven for about 45 minutes. Then i let the bread cool down with the oven door open.

Tip: it tastes best when the individual slices are roasted.

WHOLE GRAIN BREAD WITH CARROTS

25 min.
Easy
2379 kcal

Ingredients

For 1 Servings

- 500 g flour (whole wheat flour)
- 2 teaspoons of dry yeast or an equivalent amount of fresh yeast
- 1 teaspoon fine salt
- 1 tablespoon honey (wild honey)
- 2 tablespoons of balsamic vinegar
- 400 ml of warm water
- 150 g bowls of cereal (flax seeds, sunflower seeds)
- 2 m. Even one or more large carrots, 1 1/2, will do, depending on your taste

Nutritional values per serving

- Kcal 2379
- Protein 76.08 g
- Fat 8.51 g
- Carbohydrate 486.27 g

PREPARATION

Working time approx. 25 minutes
Cooking time/cooking time approx. 1 hour
Total time approx. 1 hour and 25 minutes

1. I make this bread according to a 3-minute bread recipe; i've only changed a few things, the principle is the same.
2. Allow the yeast is first dissolved in warm water, and then honey, salt, vinegar, and cereals are added. When the honey has melted, add the flour and mix well. Peel the carrots and cut them into skinny slices so that they are nice and juicy. Add the carrots to the rest of the dough and knead again well. If the dough is still very sticky, add more flour until the dough steps well and is no longer sticky.

3. Grease a bread pan with butter or margarine and add the batter. You have to put everything in the oven at 200 ° c for 60 minutes (do not preheat!). I still put a small bowl of water in the oven; it has a nice crispy crust. After 60 minutes, take the bread out of the oven, take it out of the mold and let it cool on a wire rack.
4. It is especially good with butter/margarine that is still warm.

HOMEMADE BREAD

20 minutes.
Normal
3537 kcal

Ingredients

For 1 Portions

- 800 g of soft wheat flour type 550
- 200 g wholemeal flour
- 1 spoon of sugar
- 1 yeast cube, (42 g)
- 1 tablespoon of salt
- 700 ml of water up to 750 ml

Nutritional values per serving

- Kcal 3537
- Protein 116.17 g
- Fat 13.35 g
- Carbohydrate 717.07 g

Preparation

Processing time of about 20 minutes.
Total time of about 20 minutes.

1. Mix both types of flour with the sugar and make a well. Dissolve the yeast in the salted water. Pour into the well. Mix the mixture well and work it with your hands until you get a homogeneous dough. Put the dough in a pan or bowl and put it in warm (not boiling) water for about 1 hour and a half.
2. It can also be covered and covered without throwing it in a warm place. The dough must be at least twice the height.
3. Put the bread dough in the oven with the mold or by hand. Bake at 200 degrees for about 1 hour.
4. The bread is done when it comes off the edge of the pan or is golden brown. (my friend, who gave me the recipe, bakes the bread in the tupperware ultra plus 5.0 l casserole. She fills the dough in the pan and puts it in warm water.

When the dough has reached the edge of the pan, she puts it in without putting the lid on. Again, the bread is done when it comes off the edge of the pan.)

BREAD IN THE PAN

15 minutes.
Easy
3434 kcal

Ingredients

For 1 Portions

- 1,000 g of soft wheat flour type 1050
- 3 teaspoons of salt
- 800 ml of water
- 1 teaspoon dry yeast

Nutritional values per serving

- Kcal 3434
- Protein 102.27 g
- Fat 10.18 g
- Carbohydrate 712.84 g

Preparation

Processing time of about 15 minutes.
Rest time about 1 day
Cooking/cooking time approx. 1 hour
Total time about 1 day 1 hour and 15 minutes

1. Mix the flour, salt, and water with the yeast (do not knead!). Cover the dough with a cloth and let it rise to room temperature. After 24 hours, knead the dough only briefly.
2. Preheat the oven and broil at 250 ° c (top/bottom heat). Pour the batter into the hot saucepan, cover with the lid (so the moisture doesn't scatter), and bake for 1 hour.
3. Let cool for a moment, and then remove the bread from the pan.

SPELLED YOGURT BREAD

10 minutes.
Easy
2994 kcal

Ingredients

For 1 Portions

- 700 g of spelled flour type 630
- 100 g rye flour
- 350 ml of warm water
- 20 g yeast
- Cut 3 tsp. Salt-
- 1 tablespoon of honey
- 150 g of yogurt

Nutritional values per serving

- Kcal 2994
- Protein 104.17 g
- Fat 19.56 g
- Carbohydrate 571.65 g

Preparation

Processing time of about 10 minutes.
The rest time of about 2 hours and 30 minutes.
Cooking/cooking time approx. 1 hour
Total time around 3 hours and 40 minutes.

1. In a mixing bowl, combine the two forms of flour. Add the remaining ingredients and mix them with your hands until a homogeneous dough forms. Cover and set aside for 90 minutes in a warm place.
2. Remove from the bowl, knead again and place in a refractory container with a lid. Cut slightly on the surface and sprinkle with a little flour. Let stand for another 60 minutes.

3. The bread is placed in the cold oven and baked at 180 ° c for 50 minutes with the lid closed. Remove the cover and continue baking at 220° c for another 7-10 minutes. Allow the bread to cool fully on a wire rack.

BREAD IN A ROMAN POT

15 minutes.
Simple
3919 kcal

Ingredients

For 1Servings

- 1,000 g wheat flour
- 500 ml buttermilk
- 2 pck. Dry yeast
- 2 tbsp quark
- 1 tbsp honey
- 3 tsp salt
- 1 egg (s)
- 2 tbsp milk
- N. B. Sunflower seeds

Nutritional Values Per Serving

- Kcal 3919
- Protein140.82 g
- Fat 25.51 g
- Carbohydrate 757.40 g

Preparation

Working time approx. 15 minutes
Cooking / baking time approx. 1 hour 20 minutes
Total time approx. 1 hour 35 minutes

1. Warm the buttermilk and milk to lukewarm. Add the yeast, honey, salt, quark and the egg and stir everything well. Pour everything slowly into the flour and stir for about 5 minutes. Then knead with your hands and shape into a loaf of bread.

2. Line the soaked römertopf with parchment paper or dust with flour and place the loaf in it. For a smoother surface, you can brush the loaf with lukewarm milk. If you like, you can also look after the loaf with sunflower seeds. I always use baking paper, as the bread loosens easily and it also makes washing up a bit easier.

3. Place the lid on the römertopf and place in the cold (!) Oven and bake at 180 ° c for 60 minutes. Then remove the lid and brown for another 20 minutes. Let the bread cool down and then enjoy.

SPELLED WALNUT BREAD

30 min.
Normal
3969 kcal

Ingredients

For 1Servings

- 400 g sourdough, (spelled sourdough)
- 400 g spelled flour, type 1050
- 300 g water
- 23 g salt
- 100 g oatmeal, fine
- 100 g walnuts
- Flour, water
- 1 tbsp syrup, (agave syrup), or honey
- Possibly.Yeast, something with young sourdough

Nutritional values per serving

- Kcal 3969
- Protein 122.41 g
- Fat 93.54 g
- Carbohydrate 645.10 g

Preparation

Working time approx. 30 minutes
Rest time approx. 1 hour 30 minutes
Cooking / baking time approx. 40 minutes
Total time approx. 2 hours 40 minutes

1. Put the walnuts in a bowl and pour boiling water over them and let them stand for 15-20 minutes, then pour off the water.
2. In the meantime, mix the sourdough, flour, salt, oat flakes, water (possibly more, depends on the firmness of the sourdough) and agave syrup, add walnuts. Now cover the dough and let it rise. About 30 - 40 minutes until the dough has doubled in volume. Then shape the loaf and place in a proofing

basket or something similar and cover again. About 30 - 40 minutes until the dough has risen visibly again.

3. Now turn out onto a prepared baking sheet, cut into a grid shape and bake at 250 ° c for 15 minutes, after 5 minutes of this time, steam. Turn the oven down to 200 ° c and bake for another 30-45 minutes (i need a little longer, well more like the bread, my oven is not exactly the newest). In between i spray the bread twice with water and after baking (fresh from the oven) again (i use a flower sprayer).

Note:

You can also bake the bread with other types of flour.

ANCIENT ROMAN BREAD

15 minutes.
Simple
505 kcal

Ingredients

For 4Servings

- 500 g flour (whole wheat flour)
- 300 ml water, lukewarm
- 4 tbsp   honey
- 20 g yeast (fresh yeast, half a cube)
- 1 teaspoon salt
- 1 onion (s), finely chopped

Nutritional values per serving

- Kcal 505
- Protein 13.44 g
- Fat 1.37 g
- Carbohydrate 107.08 g

Preparation

Working time approx. 15 minutes
Total time approx. 15 minutes

1. Mix all ingredients, crumble the yeast into the mixture. Knead into a bread dough either in the food processor or by hand. Shape into a loaf and let rise in a warm place (possibly in a very weakly heated oven, about 20 minutes). Then brush the top of the loaf with honey (gives a great crust) and bake at 200 degrees (convection) for about 45 minutes (the bread rises better if you put a shallow bowl of water in the oven).

2. The bread recipe was used by the roman legionaries when they were at war. Everyone was given a certain ration of flour, the bread was then varied with other ingredients that were currently available. In addition to the onion variant, i've also added apples and carrots (leave out the onion). The imagination knows no limits. Herbs, pepper or leek also go very well.

GLUTEN-FREE HAZELNUT BREAD

20 minutes.
Normal
2293 kcal

Ingredients

For1 servings

- 400 g flour, gluten-free, light
- 100 g of chopped hazelnuts
- 1 teaspoon salt
- 1 cube of fresh yeast
- 360 ml of warm water
- 1 tablespoon of rapeseed oil
- 1 handful of whole hazelnuts

Nutritional values per serving

- Kcal 2293
- Protein 67.34 g
- Fat 92.79 g
- Carbohydrate 291.82 g

Preparation

Working time approx. 20 minutes
Standby time approx. 1 hour
Cooking time/cooking time approx. 40 minutes
Total time approx. 2 hours

1. Mix the flour, hazelnuts, and salt in a bowl. Dissolve the yeast in warm water and add to the flour along with the oil. Let everything be kneaded well in the food processor. Finally, mix in the whole walnuts.
2. Grease a loaf pan and pour the batter into it with a wet spoon. At this point, brush the paste with a little oil and cover it with a piece of cling film that is also oiled. Let the dough rise in the kitchen until it reaches the edge of the pan.

3. Preheat the oven by circulating air to 230 degrees. Bake the bread for 10 minutes, then set the temperature to 200 degrees. Bake at this temperature for 20 minutes, brush the bread with oil, and bake for another 10 minutes.

LOW CARB COTTAGE CHEESE BREAD

10 minutes.
easy

Ingredients

<u>For1 serving</u>

- 2 large eggs
- 500 g low-fat quark
- 300 g of ground almonds
- 50 g chia seeds
- 5 g baking powder
- 1 teaspoon psyllium
- 1 teaspoon salt

Preparation

1. Working time approx. 10 minutes.
2. Cooking time/cooking time approx. 1 hour
3. Total time approx. 1 hour and 10 minutes
4. Mix every ingredient and bake at 180 degrees for about an hour.

CIABATTA (1 LARGE LOAF OR TWO SMALL ONES)

30 minutes.
Normal
1035 kcal

Ingredients

For 1 serving

- 300 g of flour, 550 (or 200 g 550 + 100 g of steam)
- 130 ml cold water
- 3 g fresh yeast - crumble into flour
- 2 g fresh yeast
- 3 g of baked malt or 1/2 teaspoon of honey
- 70 ml cold water
- 6 grams of salt

Nutritional values per serving

- Kcal 1035
- Protein 30.55 g
- Fat 3.14 g
- Carbohydrate 214.82 g

Preparation

Working time approx. 30 minutes.
Rest time approx. 21 hours
Total time approx. 21 hours and 30 minutes

1. Lightly knead 300 g of flour, 130 g of water, and 3 g of yeast and form a ball (the dough is substantial), place in a large enough bowl, and cover with aluminum foil for 18 to 20 hours at 18 to 22 ° C.

Then:

2. Dissolve 2 g of yeast, 3 g of baked malt, or ½ teaspoon of honey in 70 g of water, add slowly and gradually to the dough, and knead so that the dough absorbs the liquid well !!!

3. (Works great with the dough hook hand mixer, my dough hook food processor had some trouble mixing the dough and water well.)
4. Put 6 g of salt in 15 g of water and add to the dough.
5. Now knead the dough with the food processor for about 15 to 20 minutes until it separates from the edge of the bowl, then let it rise in a covered bowl * for about 40 to 60 minutes until it has grown well.
6. Remove the dough from the bowl's rim and place it on a floured surface, preferably on well-floured parchment paper, as the dough is very soft and difficult to transport.
7. Flour the dough's body and give it a slight shape, don't knead the dough anymore !! o Divide the dough in half with a spatula and gently shape it.
8. Cover with a kitchen towel and bake for about 40-50 minutes (depending on the temperature), then in an oven preheated to 250 ° with steam.

- 250 ° - 10 min.
- 220 ° - 10 min.
- And more. 10 minutes. At 220-200 °, depending on the tan.

* .... You can put the dough in a bowl greased with olive oil, it is better to soften it later, and the dough also receives a splash of oil.

SEVEN DAYS OF BREAD

30 minutes.
intelligent
2097 kcal

Ingredients

<u>For 1 serving</u>

- For the dough: (total preliminary dough)
- 1 cup of wheat flour, type 550
- 5 heaped tablespoons of wheat flour, type 550
- 2 tablespoons of dry yeast
- 1 tablespoon of wheat flour, heaped (wholemeal)
- 1 cup of warm water
- For the dough: (main dough)
- 3 cups / n soft wheat flour type 550
- ½ cup of wholemeal flour
- 1 tablespoon of dry yeast
- 1 tablespoon of sugar
- 1 tablespoon of salt
- 1 cup of warm water

Nutritional values per serving

- Kcal 2097
- Protein 73.17 g
- Fat 6.32 g
- Carbohydrate 424.95 g

Preparation

Processing time about 30 minutes
Rest time about seven days 1 hour
Cooking/cooking time about 40 minutes
Total time about seven days 2 hours 10 minutes
The cup should have a volume of 150g.

1. Day one:

2. 1 cup soft wheat flour style 550, 2 teaspoons dry yeast, 1 cup warm water Combine all of the ingredients in a mixing bowl and cover tightly with the lid. Add one heaping tablespoon of form 550 flour to the dough in the evening.
3. Day two:
4. In the morning, add one heaping tablespoon of type 550 flour, and in the evening, add two heaping tablespoons of type 550 flour.
5. Day three:
6. In the morning, add one heaping tablespoon of wholemeal flour, and in the evening, one heaping tablespoon of 550 flour.
7. Day four and five:
8. Just mix the pre-batter once a day, then place it in the refrigerator on the fifth day's evening, where it can be kept until the sixth day.
9. seventh day:
10. Combine 3 cups form 550 flour, 1/2 cup whole wheat flour, and one tablespoon dry yeast with salt and sugar in a big mixing bowl. Combine the dry ingredients with the pre-batter (mix first!) In a separate bowl, combine 1 cup warm water and knead well to form a smooth batter. Allow 30 minutes to rest in a warm spot.
11. Then, on a floured work surface, shape the bread briefly and gently, then position it on a prepared baking sheet or in a pan. The bread will rise a little higher as the oven heats up to 200 degrees.
12. The bread will take about 30-40 minutes to bake. The bread should then be covered and allowed to cool on a kitchen counter.

5 CEREALS - FLAKES – BREAD

20 minutes.
Normal
2883 kcal

Ingredients

<u>For 1 serving</u>

- 400 g of pasta (rye sourdough) and 100 g of 5-grain flakes
- 85 ml of water to soak the flakes
- 225 g flour (rye flour)
- 125 g flour (wheat flour)
- 200 ml of warm water
- 1 tablespoon. Salt and possibly two tablespoons of oven malt
- 80 g of sesame or other seeds according to your wishes

Nutritional values per serving

- Kcal 2883
- Protein 80.22 g
- Fat 86.58 g
- Carbohydrate 431.27 g

Preparation

Processing time about 20 minutes
Rest time about 2 hours
Total time about 2 hours and 20 minutes

1. Soak the flakes in water for about 10 minutes before using. Then, using all of the ingredients, make a relatively soft bread dough and let it rest for about 20 minutes.
2. Re-knead the dough and position it in a loaf pan or pan dusted with seeds. Sprinkle with seeds if needed, and set aside for 1.5 to 2 hours.
3. Bake for 90 minutes at 175 degrees Celsius on high and low heat.

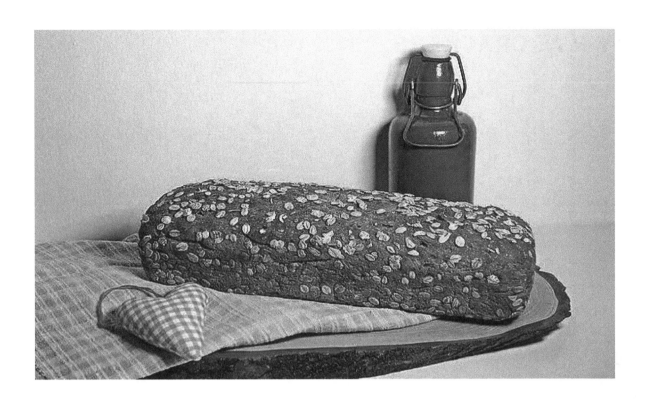

CRISPY RYE CRACKERS

20 minutes.
easy
2783 kcal

Ingredients

<u>For 1 serving</u>

- 1 yeast cube
- 450 ml of warm water
- 500 g of flour (spelled or whole)
- 50 g of sunflower seeds
- 50 g of sesame seeds
- 50 g flaxseed
- 2 teaspoons of salt
- 2 tablespoons vinegar (fruit vinegar) or bread drink
- Fat for the form

Nutritional values per serving

- Kcal 2783
- Protein 98.67 g
- Fat 86.06 g
- Carbohydrate 394.39 g

Preparation

Approximate working time: 20 minutes
Approximate total time: 20 minutes

1. Combine the yeast and the water in a mixing bowl. Combine all of the remaining ingredients and stir well. Place the casserole in a cold oven that has been greased. Allow the bread to rise but do not allow it to rise too much. Bake at 200°C for 60 minutes or 170°C with hot air for 50 minutes.
2. If required, remove the bread from the pan and bake for another 10 minutes. Cereals may be left out or substituted (raisins, almonds, walnuts). Dry yeast may also be used.

CHIA PROTEIN BREAD

15 minutes.
easy
1881 kcal

Ingredients

For 1 serving

- 250 g oat bran
- 40 g of wheat bran
- 2 tablespoons chia seeds
- 5 eggs
- 1 package baking powder
- 500 g low-fat quark
- Bread spice mix
- 3 prices go up

Nutritional values per serving

- Kcal 1881
- Protein 150.32 g
- Fat 56.15 g
- Carbohydrate 183.66 g

Preparation

Approximate working time: 15 minutes
Approximate prep time/cooking time: 40 minutes
Approximate total time: 55 minutes

1. Preheat the oven to 180 degrees Fahrenheit.
2. Except for one tablespoon of chia seeds, combine all ingredients thoroughly.
3. Pour the batter into a medium-sized baking sheet lined with parchment paper. Cover the dough with the remaining chia seeds and gently press them in.
4. Bake on the center rack for 40 minutes at 180 degrees.
5. After cooking, remove the bread from the pan and let it cool on a wire rack.

BREAD BAKED WITH BEER

5 minutes.
easy
3242 kcal

Ingredients

<u>For 1 Portions</u>

- 600 grams of flour
- 500 ml of malt beer or other beer
- 1 on / n of baking powder
- 2 teaspoons of salt
- 1 ½ cup / n of sunflower seeds or other items, e.g., Eg fried onions

Nutritional values per serving

- Kcal 3242
- Protein 111.03 gr
- Fat 54.92 g
- Carbohydrate 552.65 g

Preparation

Approximate working time: 5 minutes
Approximate prep time/cooking time: 55 minutes
Approximate total time: 1 hour

1. Combine all of the ingredients and shape into a loaf. Add the sunflower seeds and a splash of water to the tip.
2. Preheat the oven to 200°F and bake for 55 minutes. On the foot, place a cup of water.
3. You should omit the cup of water if you're using Ultra Tupperware. After that, bake for 35 minutes with the lid on and 15 minutes without.

NAHAN BREAD

20 minutes.
easy
1951 kcal

Ingredients

For 1 Portions

- 190 ml of warm water
- 2 tablespoons of oil (sunflower oil)
- 1 teaspoon of honey
- 4 tablespoons of yogurt
- 1 teaspoon of salt
- 450 g flour (type 550)
- 20 g of yeast (alternatively 1 teaspoon of dry yeast)
- Flour for the work surface

Nutritional values per serving

- Kcal 1951
- Protein 59.82 g
- Fat 23.70 g
- Carbohydrate 364.31 g

Preparation

Processing time is about 20 minutes.
1 hour of rest time

1. About an hour and a half to an hour and a half to an hour and a half to an
2. Place the ingredients on the bread maker's baking tray in the order listed (water, oil, honey, yogurt, salt, flour, and yeast) (BBA). Begin by running the "Dough" software.
3. Lay the dough on a floured work surface and knead for 3 minutes once the kneading program is done. After that, divide the mixture into eight equal bits. With a lightly floured rolling pin, roll out the dough parts to a thickness of about 1/2 cm. Place four loaves of naan bread per baking sheet that has been lined with parchment paper. Cook for about 20 minutes, covered with a damp cloth.

4. Preheat the grill to its highest setting. Take the tea towel from each piece of bread and grill for 2-3 minutes, or until golden spots appear on the surface. Then turn the bread over and toast it for a few seconds. Serve right away.

5. Glitter magic for bread

FIVE MINUTES

5 minutes
easy
77 kcal

Ingredients

<u>For 1 Portions</u>

- 200 ml of water
- 1 tablespoon of food starch
- 1 tablespoon of salt

Nutritional values per serving

- Kcal 77
- Protein 0.09 g
- Fat 0.02 g
- Carbohydrate 18.90 g

Preparation

Processing time is about 5 minutes.
Approximately 5 minutes total

1. This agent gives the bread its distinct luster. Since it resembles mud, I affectionately refer to it as magical mud.
2. I provided this recipe here because I get asked about it a lot. It's coated on my bread after it's baked (15 minutes for me) and then again 15 minutes before it's baked. You can see the bread covered with it in my photo album, especially the Delphinella wheat bread and my double-baked rye bread, which you can recognize as being particularly good.
3. To avoid lumps, thoroughly combine all of the ingredients. Bring it to a boil, then remove from the heat and pour into a bottle.
4. Since I bake almost every day, a jar like this will last about ten days in the fridge.

TWO MINUTES OF BREAD

45 min.
easy

Ingredients

- for 1 Portions
- 500 g of flour
- 1 sachet of baking powder
- 1 teaspoon of salt
- 1 can of onion (s) (fried onions)
- ½ liter of malt beer

Preparation

Processing time is about 45 minutes.
Approximately 45 minutes total

1. In a mixing dish, combine the flour and baking powder. Combine all of the remaining ingredients in a batter. In a silicone tub, pour the batter.
2. For around 40-45 minutes in a preheated oven at 180° C.
3. Remove from the oven, set aside to cool, and then chop.

BREAD WITH SEMOLINA AND A TOUCH OF REFINED OLIVE OIL

20 minutes.
easy
1734 kcal

Ingredients

For 1 portions

- 230 g of flour
- 195 g fine-grained semolina
- 2 teaspoons dry yeast
- 1 teaspoon salt
- 240 ml of warm water
- 1 tablespoon olive oil plus an additional amount
- 2 teaspoons of herbs to taste
- butter

Nutritional values per serving

- Kcal 1734
- Protein 0.04 g
- Fat 31.19 g
- Carbohydrate 305.51 g

Preparation

Approximate working time: 20 minutes
3 hours of rest is recommended.
Approximate total time: 3 hours and 20 minutes

1. One is 24 cm long. Brush the bottom of the pan (I always use a round glass cake) with butter and one tablespoon of olive oil.
2. Mix the flour, semolina, and salt together, then soak the dry yeast in a small amount of warm water for a few minutes. Then add the rest of the water to the flour mixture and mix for 3-4 minutes with the planetary mixer. Cover and steep for 1 to 2 hours in a warm location.

3. Place the dough on a pastry board and knead it briefly before shaping it into a ball and gently pressing it until it is the size of the pan. Place the dough in the prepared pan, cover, and set aside for 1 hour or until it is well-risen.

4. Preheat the oven to 190 degrees in the meantime. With your fingers, make a few indentations in the sourdough, then drizzle a little oil over it. Preheat the oven to 350°F and bake for 30-40 minutes, or until golden brown.

5. Withdraw and, if desired, consult Dr. Sprinkle with spices, then unmold and cool on a rack for 5 minutes.

FRIED ONIONS AND MALT BREAD

10 minutes.
easy
2499 kcal

Ingredients

For 1 Portions

- 500g of flour
- 500 ml of malt beer
- 1 package baking powder
- 1 teaspoon salt
- 125g roasted onions

Nutritional values per serving

- Kcal 2499
- Protein 72.42 g
- Fat 23.50 g
- Carbohydrate 477.76 g

Preparation

Working time is about ten minutes.
Approximate prep time/cooking time: 50 minutes
Approximate total time: 1 hour

1. To make the dough, combine all of the ingredients in a food processor. Fill a greased or parchment-lined baking sheet halfway with batter.
2. Preheat the oven to 190 degrees Celsius in a fan oven. Bake the bread for 30 minutes at 190 degrees Celsius, then for 20 minutes at 170 degrees Celsius. Allow to cool fully on a wire rack.

YOGURT BREAD

15 minutes.
easy
1999 kcal

Ingredients

For 1 Portions

- 500g of flour
- 200 ml milk
- 150 g of natural yogurt
- 21 g yeast, fresh or similar
- 1 package dry yeast
- 14 g of salt
- 8 grams of sugar

Nutritional values per serving

- Kcal 1999
- Protein 67.38 g
- Fat 17.91 g
- Carbohydrate 380.63 g

Preparation

Approximate working time: 15 minutes
2 hours of rest is recommended.
Approximate total time: 2 hours and 15 minutes

1. In a bottle, dissolve the yeast in half the warm milk, then add the salt and stir well. Allow 30 minutes to pass after setting the glass aside.
2. Then, in a mixing bowl, combine all of the remaining ingredients, add the yeast, salt, and milk, and thoroughly combine it. Knead for at least 5 minutes, ideally 7-10 minutes, vigorously. Cover the dough and set it aside for at least an hour and a half to rest. It's natural for the dough to be a little sticky. As a result, just add more flour if the batter is almost runny, which should not be the case when using standard wheat flour.

3. Knead the dough as much as possible after it has rested. Place the dough in a skillet or a special frying pan and cover for 30 to 45 minutes, or until the bread has doubled in volume. If you like, you can cut the surface several times.

4. Place the pan in the preheated oven and bake at 200 ° C on high/low heat once it has risen. Reduce the temperature to 180 ° C after 5 minutes and bake for another 40 minutes. It is preferable to cover the bread with aluminum foil or reduce the temperature if the bread becomes too dark. It's worth noting that each oven heats up differently, so the cooking time can differ.

5. Yogurt bread is extremely soft and stays fresh for an extended period of time.

SPELLED AND RYE BREAD

25 min.
easy
3028 kcal

Ingredients

For 1 Portions

- 40 g of yeast
- ½ liter of hot water
- 1 teaspoon of brown sugar (also brown sugar)
- 40 g quark (low fat quark)
- 300 g flour (type 1150)
- 350 g flour (wholemeal spelled)
- 2 teaspoons of salt
- Depending on your needs, 100 g of sunflower or pumpkin seeds or pine nuts, etc.
- Possibly. Fat for the shape
- Possibly. Flour for the mold

Nutritional values per serving

- Kcal 3028
- Protein 111.01 g
- Fat 45.57 g
- Carbohydrate 529.49 g

Preparation

Processing time is about 25 minutes.
Total time is about 25 minutes.

1. Combine the yeast, water, sugar, and quark in a mixing bowl. Gradually incorporate the flour, salt, and cereals of your choosing into the batter. To make a homogeneous mixture, combine all of the ingredients in a mixing bowl. Allow it to sit for 30 minutes in a warm spot.
2. Dust a 30 cm baking pan with flour and line it with parchment paper or fat. Fill the mold with the mixture, gently cut it with a knife, and roll it out with water.

If desired, you can top with additional seeds. In a cold oven, place the bread on the lower rack.

3. Preheat oven to 220°C and bake for 50 minutes.
4. To prevent the bread from being too dark, cover it for the last 20 minutes.

SPELLED YOGURT BREAD

10 min.
easy
2994 kcal

Ingredients

For 1 Portions

- 700 g spelled flour type 630
- 100 g of rye flour
- 350 ml of warm water
- 20 g of yeast
- 3 teaspoons of sliced salt
- 1 tablespoon of honey
- 150 g of yogurt

Nutritional values per serving

- Kcal 2994
- Protein 104.17 g
- Fat 19.56 g
- Carbohydrate 571.65 g

Preparation

- It takes about 25 minutes to complete the processing.
- The total time is approximately 25 minutes.
- In a mixing bowl, combine the yeast, water, sugar, and quark. Gradually stir in the flour, salt, and cereals of your choice until the batter is smooth. In a mixing bowl, add all of the ingredients to produce a homogeneous mixture. Allow it to sit in a warm place for 30 minutes.
- Top a 30 cm baking sheet with parchment paper or fat and dust it with flour. Fill the mold halfway with the mixture, cut it with a knife gently, and roll it out with water. Additional seeds can be sprinkled on top if desired. Place the bread on the bottom rack of a cold oven.
- Preheat the oven to 220 degrees Fahrenheit and bake for 50 minutes.
- Cover the bread to keep it from getting too dark.

- The bread is put in a cold oven and baked for 50 minutes at 180 degrees Celsius with the lid closed. Remove the cover and continue baking at 220° C for another 7-10 minutes. Allow the bread to cool fully on a wire rack.

PIZZA BREAD FOR THE BAKERY

15 minutes.
easy
1210 kcal

Ingredients

<u>For 1 Portions</u>

- 110 ml of water
- 110 ml of tomatoes, success
- 1 tablespoon of olive oil
- 1 spoon of sugar
- 1 teaspoon salt
- 300 g of soft wheat flour type 1050
- 1 teaspoon dry yeast
- 4 teaspoons dried Italian herbs
- 1 pinch of granulated garlic

Nutritional values per serving

- Kcal 1210
- Protein 35.01 g
- Fat 10.45 g
- Carbohydrate 237.26 g

Preparation

Approximate working time: 15 minutes
Approximate total time: 15 minutes

1. This bread is best baked in a bread maker. Pour all of the ingredients into the bowl one by one, starting with the standard program and ending with the light golden.
2. If you don't have a bread maker, you'll have to test how long it's been in the oven. However, since it is a small loaf (although it can be turned into a larger one!), you won't need to bake it for very long. With butter, it's even better!

EAR OF BREAD

20 minutes.
Normal
1208 kcal

Ingredients

For 2 Portions

- 400 g of wheat flour
- 100 g rye flour
- 350 ml of water
- 10 g of salt
- 15 g fresh yeast
- 200 g of grated mozzarella
- 150 g of smoked ham, thinly sliced

Nutritional values per serving

- Kcal 1208
- Protein 58.07 g
- Fat 26.37 g
- Carbohydrate 179.95 g

Preparation

Approximate working time: 20 minutes
30 minutes of rest is recommended.
Approximate prep time/cooking time: 30 minutes
Approximate total time: 1 hour and 20 minutes

1. Knead the dough thoroughly with soft wheat flour, rye flour, water, yeast, and salt. If possible, add a little more flour.
2. Allow the dough to rest for 30 minutes. Knead once more and split into two equal parts. Preheat the oven to 180 degrees Celsius.
3. Sprinkle grated cheese over a piece of dough that has been rolled into a rectangle, leaving the top edge free. Starting at the bottom, lay the ham lengthwise. The ham can only cover about 2/3 of the dough's surface. Starting

with the ham's hand, roll it up. Pinch the dough's edges together tightly and place the seam upside down.

4. Position the rolls on a parchment-paper-lined baking sheet. Cut 2/3 of the rolls at a 45° angle to the kitchen counter with kitchen scissors. It's necessary: don't cut all the way through! To keep the ear's form, separate individual segments once to the right and once to the left.

5. Put the two ears of wheat on a parchment-lined baking sheet and bake the cakes until golden brown. I add about 250 mL of water to the bottom of the oven to steam vigorously. Remove the ears from the oven after around 25 to 30 minutes, when they are cool and light brown.

6. Anyone can tear off a slice of the ears, which can be eaten hot or cold.

7. The filling is merely a recommendation and can be replaced with anything you want, such as salami slices. It's important not to dice the filling too finely. Otherwise, cutting the roll would be difficult.

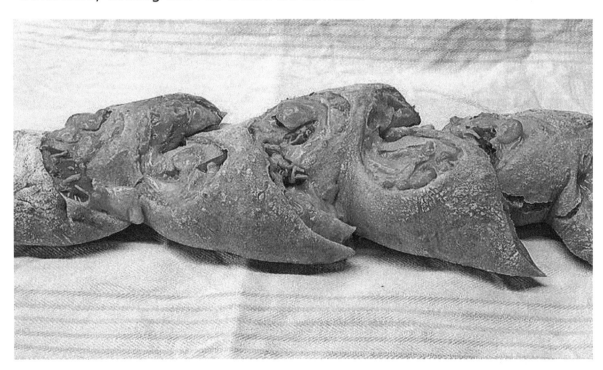

CHEESE BREAD

15 minutes.
Easy
1582 kcal

Ingredients

<u>For 1 Portions</u>

- 1 cup of milk
- 2 cups / n flour
- 1 package baking powder
- 2 cups of grated cheese
- 1 pinch of salt
- Fat for the form

Nutritional values per serving

- Kcal 1582
- Protein 58.58 g
- Fat 76.81 g
- Carbohydrate 160.71 g

Preparation

Approximate working time: 15 minutes
Approximate total time: 15 minutes

Combine all of the ingredients in a finely greased skillet. Preheat the oven to 190 degrees Celsius. Time: 25 minutes

BREAD WITH OLIVES AND DRIED TOMATOES

20 minutes.
normal
1424 kcal

Ingredients

For 2 servings

- 640 g flour
- 21 g yeast (fresh)
- 1 ½ teaspoon of salt
- 3 tablespoons of olive oil
- 350 ml water (warm)
- 130 g pitted black olives
- 200 g dried tomato (s), pickled in olive oil

Nutritional values per serving

- Kcal 1424
- Protein 39.82 g
- Fat 28.08 g
- Carbohydrate 244.87 g

Preparation

Approximate working time: 20 minutes
Approximate rest time: 2 hours
Approximate total time: 2 hours and 20 minutes

1. Create a source in the middle of the flour in a dish. In a cup, combine the yeast and warm water, then pour it into the spring. With your finger, add something to the flour. Knead in the salt, olive oil, and water until an elastic dough forms. You can need a little more water depending on the flour.
2. Knead the dough for about 5 minutes on a lightly floured work surface. Then put it back in the container and leave it to grow for about an hour in a dark, covered area. The volume should be increased by twofold.

3. Meanwhile, cut the tomatoes into small pieces, being careful not to cut them too short. I still cut them in half and quarters; cutting the olives will save you time. When you knead them, they crack.

4. Line a baking sheet with parchment paper and split the dough into two equal parts after briefly kneading it. Return a little to the cup, along with half of the olives and tomatoes, and thoroughly mix it together.

5. Dust the dough with flour, roll it out into a circle, and place it in the tub. Do the same thing for the other half of the dough. Flatten the two round dough parts slightly, flour them, and cut them in half with a sharp knife. Cover and set aside for another hour in a warm place. Here the dough should have grown significantly again.

6. In the meantime, preheat the oven to 220 degrees and bake the loaves for 25 to 30 minutes or until golden brown. Take out of the oven and let cool completely on a wire rack.

SWEETBREAD

30 minutes.
Normal
2982 kcal

Ingredients

For 1 servings

- 500g flour
- 50 grams of sugar
- 150 g quark
- 175 ml milk
- 60 g butter
- 1 tablespoon of applesauce
- 1 teaspoon of salt
- 21 g fresh yeast OR
- 1 packet of yeast (dry yeast)
- 100 g raisins, just enough

Nutritional values per serving

- Kcal 2982
- Protein 82.40 g
- Fat 69.56 g
- Carbohydrate 491.87 g

Preparation

Approximate working time: 30 minutes
Approximate rest time: 3 hours
Approximate total time: 3 hours and 30 minutes

1. I never make a pre-dough by itself because I think it's unnecessary, particularly for "light" bread or baked goods. I continue to make delicious baked goods.
2. However, if you want to do one, you can, as you are aware.
3. Combine the milk, yeast, and salt in a mixing bowl and set aside to rest for a few minutes.
4. In a cup, combine the flour, applesauce (surprise, surprise), soft but not too runny butter, and quark.

5. Combine the yeast, milk, and sugar in a mixing bowl and knead for 5-10 minutes, using both the pump and your hands. You must knead the dough for a long time until it forms a smooth dough and the ingredients are thoroughly combined. OK

6. Finally, if necessary, add the raisins and knead briefly again.

7. Enable the yeast to rest independently for at least 1-2 hours by covering it and placing it in a warm spot.

8. (Of course, you can do all of this in the BBA; just make sure the raisins are added last.)

9. After standing or raising the yeast dough, vigorously beat it again and knead it thoroughly.

10. Place the dough in a loaf pan and let it rest for another 30 minutes in a warm place.

11. Bake the bread for 45 minutes in a preheated oven at 180 ° C or 165 ° C in a fan oven.

12. (Due to the fact that each oven heats up differently, it can take a little longer.) Ensure that the bread does not get too dark.)

13. Bread is a soft bread that can be eaten for breakfast or as a snack in the afternoon.

14. The tablespoon of applesauce creates a delicious, melted crumb that prevents the mare from drying out and keeps it fresh for several days. As a result, no egg should ever be added to the dough.

15. The sugar content can be decreased, just like raisins, even though I've already weighed it at 50-100 g.

16. You can completely avoid them if you don't like them.

LOW-CARB BREAD

20 minutes.
easy

Ingredients

For 1 Portions

- 500 g of low-fat quark
- eggs
- 2 teaspoons of salt
- 200 g of carrots
- 2 tablespoons of chopped almonds
- 4 tablespoons of ground flaxseed
- 50 g of bran (wheat bran)
- 250 g bran (oat bran)
- 4 tablespoons of sunflower or pumpkin seeds
- 1 sachet of baking powder
- Fat for the shape
- Oat flakes or sunflower seeds, or pumpkin seeds for sprinkling

Preparation

Processing time is about 20 minutes.
1 hour of cooking/cooking time
About an hour and a half to an hour and a half to an hour and a half to an

1. Preheat the oven to 200°F, then preheat again.
2. To make the dough, grate the carrots and mix them with the rest of the ingredients.
3. A 12-inch pan should be well greased. Pour the batter into the pan evenly. More sunflower seeds or oatmeal can be sprinkled on top of the dough.
4. Bake the bread for 60 minutes on the middle rack.
5. After baking, remove the bread from the pan as soon as possible and cool completely. Wrap the bread in bread paper and place it in the refrigerator. It keeps for 4-5 days and tastes delicious.
6. My recommendation is to butter the bread and then season it with salt and chives.

HERBAL CREAM CHEESE – BREAD

20 minutes.
Normal
3134 kcal

Ingredients

For 1 Portions

- 700 g of flour
- 200 g of herb cream cheese
- 42 g of yeast
- 1 tablespoon of sugar
- 2 teaspoons of salt
- 250 ml of water, possibly a little more
- Cumin seeds to sprinkle
- Milk for brushing

Nutritional values per serving

- Kcal 3134
- Protein 103.95 g
- Fat 57.21 g
- Carbohydrate 536.64 g

Preparation

Processing time is about 20 minutes.
1 hour of standby time
About an hour and a half to an hour and a half to an hour and a half to an

1. Knead the ingredients until a smooth yeast dough forms, then cover and set aside for 35 minutes to rise.
2. Cut the dough into three equal parts and shape them into sticks. Arrange them on a parchment-paper-lined baking sheet. Cover and set aside for another 15-20 minutes to infuse.
3. Spread the milk on top and sprinkle the cumin seeds on top. Preheat oven to 200°F and bake for 30 minutes.

TAJINE – BREAD

60 min.
Normal
165 kcal

Ingredients

<u>For 12 °Portions</u>

- 300 ml of warm water
- 1 teaspoon of salt, heaped
- 1 cube of fresh brewer's yeast
- ½ cup of oil (olive oil)
- 400 g of flour (approx.)

Nutritional values per serving

- Kcal 165
- Protein 3.85 g
- Fat 6.00 gr
- Carbohydrate 23.68 g

Preparation

Work time is approximately 1 hour.
1 hour of standby time
Approximately 2 hours total

1. It's a Tunisian recipe that can be used in various forms in North Africa. In a big mixing bowl, combine the water and salt. Add the lumpy yeast (or 2 p. dry yeast if you prefer). However, it takes longer to mature!). Using a hand mixer, combine all of the ingredients (if not available, hand mixer). Pour in the grease. As required, add the flour. The dough should have a much softer consistency than the pizza dough. It's important that the dough isn't too stiff or dry. If not, it will rise slowly and be difficult to knead.

2. Allow the dough to double in size by covering it and allowing it to rise for at least two hours. Depending on the form of yeast used and the consistency of the dough, this can take a long time. Form the dough into balls that are about the size of your hand, flatten them slightly, and place them on a floured baking

sheet. Cover with a damp cloth (not wet!!!) and set aside to rise. Please do not place the balls too close together, as they will only open 1/3 of the way! Then, on a large plate with a puddle of olive oil, roll the dough balls into a flat cake (it should look like a pancake). In a well-preheated pan without oil, fry until golden brown on both sides at level 2.5. It needs to be served hot!

FLOURLESS BREAD

10 mins.
Normal

Ingredients

For 1 Servings

- 290 g of oats
- 270 g sunflower seeds
- 180 g of flaxseed
- 65 g sesame seeds
- 65 g pumpkin seeds
- 4 teaspoons of chia seeds
- 8 tablespoons of psyllium husk
- 2 tablespoons of sea salt
- 2 tablespoons of agave syrup
- 6 tablespoons of oil
- 700 ml of warm water

Preparation

Approximate working time: 10 minutes
Approximate cooking time: 1 hour
Approximate total time: 1 hour and 10 minutes

1. Both of the dry ingredients are ground in a blender before being combined in a mixing bowl. After that, add the remaining ingredients. Now, using a food processor, thoroughly combine all of the ingredients until a dough is shaped that is no longer sticky. Using parchment paper, line a 12-inch loaf sheet. Then pour the "batter" into the pan and hold it down with a spoon.
2. The dough is immediately placed in the oven at 175 degrees Celsius. Remove the bread from the pan and turn it over on the baking paper once it has turned golden on top. This is how a loaf of bread is made. Cooking time is about 60 minutes.It's finished when the bread is dark enough and hollow to the touch.

SMALL, LOW-CARBOHYDRATE NUT BREAD

10 mins.
Normal
2306 kcal

Ingredients

For 1 Servings

- 50 g sunflower seeds
- 25 g wheat bran
- 25 g flaxseed flour
- 25 g almond sticks or chopped almonds
- 50 g chia seeds
- 50 g of chopped almonds
- 250 g of low-fat quark
- 1 heaping teaspoon of baking powder or baking powder with tartar
- 1 egg (s)
- 1 protein

Nutritional values per serving

- Kcal 2306
- Protein 141.39 g
- Fat 152.50 g
- Carbohydrate 45.56 g

Preparation

Working time approx. 10 minutes
Rest time approx. 15 minutes
Cooking time approx. 40 minutes
Total time approx. 1 hour 5 minutes

1. Mix the dry ingredients, then gradually add the other ingredients and knead well until a dough forms—Preheat the oven to 200 degrees. Let the dough soak in the bowl for about 15 minutes, then it solidifies.

2. Form a loaf, place it on a parchment-lined baking sheet, cover with seeds if necessary, and press down. Bake the dough for about 40 minutes at 200 degrees.

3. Different types of nuts can be used depending on your taste. The bread stays fresh in the refrigerator for at least one week. Sure, it tastes best fresh or lightly roasted.

QUICK BREAD + DELICIOUS

15 minutes.
Normal
1836 kcal

Ingredients

<u>For 1 Servings</u>

- 500 g type 405 soft wheat flour
- 1 point dry yeast
- 375 ml of warm water
- 3 tablespoons of yogurt
- 1 teaspoon of salt
- ½ teaspoon of sugar
- 1 teaspoon pepper from the mill
- 1 tablespoon of dried chives
- 1 tablespoon of dried parsley

Nutritional values per serving

- Kcal 1836
- Protein 56.91 g
- Fat 9.31 g
- Carbohydrate 370.33 g

Preparation

Approximate working time: 15 minutes
Approximate cooking time: 50 minutes
1 hour and 5 minutes is the approximate total time.

1. Combine the flour, yeast, sugar, salt, pepper, oat flakes, spices, yogurt, and water in a mixing bowl and knead until smooth. Allow to rest for 5 minutes before kneading briefly again.
2. Pour the sauce onto a parchment-lined baking sheet and bake for 50 minutes at 200° C in a non-preheated oven. Remove the bread from the pan and put it on the grill for the last 5 minutes. This will also hold the bottom crispy.
3. Simply smother your dinner in butter or a spicy paste!

STYRIAN PUMPKIN SEED BREAD WITH PUMPKIN SEED OIL

20 minutes.
Normal
2443 kcal

Ingredients

For 1Portions

- 450 g of spelled flour
- 1 tip of dry yeast
- 1 teaspoon of salt
- 1 teaspoon of the bread spice mixture
- 2 tablespoons of ground pumpkin seeds
- 100 g of whole pumpkin seeds
- 350 ml of warm water
- 3 tablespoons of pumpkin seed oil

Nutritional values per serving

- Kcal 2443
- Protein 100.29 g
- Fat 82.86 g
- Carbohydrate 309.90 g

Preparation

Processing time is about 20 minutes.
1 hour of standby time
1 hour of cooking/cooking time
Around 2 hours and 20 minutes total.

1. Combine all of the dry ingredients in a large mixing bowl. Fill the container with water and seed oil. Knead the dough before it falls out of the bowl. Allow 30 minutes for resting.
2. Sprinkle ground pumpkin seeds over the batter in a greased pan. Allow another 30 minutes for resting.

3. Using a brush, wet the area. Preheat the oven to 220 degrees Fahrenheit. In the oven, place a bowl of water. After 10 minutes, return to 180 degrees. And bake for an hour in total.

4. Do the "success test" after the cooking time has passed; if the bread sounds hollow when tapped, it has cooked thoroughly. Remove the bread from the mold, spread it with a teaspoon of seed oil and a tablespoon of hot water, and set it aside to cool.

WALNUT – BREAD

45 min.
normal
4495 kcal

Ingredients

<u>For 1 Portions</u>

- 250 g sourdough (natural ripe rye yeast)
- 250 g flour (wholemeal flour)
- 250 g of soft wheat flour type 1050
- 10 g of fresh brewer's yeast
- 500 ml of warm water
- 330 g of flour (wholemeal rye flour)
- 20 g of salt
- 1 tablespoon of honey
- 1 m of potatoes, floury cooking
- 100 g of chopped walnuts

Nutritional values per serving

- Kcal 4495
- Protein 126.03 gr
- Fat 84.03 gr
- Carbohydrate 793.42 g

Preparation

1. It takes about 45 minutes to complete the processing.
2. Rest time is about 4 hours.
3. The total time is approximately 4 hours and 45 minutes.
4. In a previous dough (quite liquid and soft), combine the whole wheat flour, wheat flour, yeast, and all of the water—about 2 hours at room temperature.
5. Boil the potatoes, then peel and mash them with a potato masher while they're still hot (or press). Allow it to cool for a few minutes.
6. Combine sourdough, pre-dough, rye flour, cinnamon, honey, and mashed potatoes in a batter. Last but not least, knead the walnuts.

7. Although the dough is solid, it is extremely sticky. There's no need to add any more flour!
8. Allow 30 minutes for resting.
9. Knead the dough once more, roll it into a ball, and put it in a floured fermentation basket. Allow 1 hour for resting.
10. Preheat oven to 250 degrees Celsius (top/bottom heat).
11. Place the bread in a hot oven (preferably on a refractory stone, but a hot pan is also possible).
12. Cook for 15 minutes at 250 degrees Celsius, or until desired browning is achieved.
13. I raised my hand. Time to cook: 45 minutes at 200-180 degrees C, turning downwards. There is enough steam for
14. 15 minutes in the beginning (about three times vigorously).
15. I use a flower sprayer for this (nozzle set to fog). Simply open the oven door a little and sprinkle vigorously (sometimes) against the oven walls (not on the bread). Rep 2-3 times more.
16. Allow the steam to escape by opening the oven door momentarily at the end of the cooking process. Cook as directed.

LOW CARB BREAD

10 mins.
Easy
1107 kcal

Ingredients

<u>For 1 servings</u>

- 50 g sunflower seeds
- 250 g of low-fat quark
- 50 g flaxseed, crushed
- 50 g wheat bran
- 50 g soy flour
- 1 teaspoon of salt
- ½ pack of baking powder
- 2 eggs)
- 2 teaspoons of milk

Nutritional values per serving

- Kcal 1107
- Protein 102.06 g
- Fat 56.86 g
- Carbohydrate 43.55 g

Preparation

Approximate working time: 10 minutes
Approximate rest time: 20 minutes
Approximate cooking time: 40 minutes
Approximate total time: 1 hour and 10 minutes

1. Preheat the oven to 200 degrees Fahrenheit.
2. Knead the ingredients thoroughly, then set aside for 20 minutes to allow the flax seeds to swell slightly.
3. Preheat the oven to 400°F and bake the bread for 40 minutes.
4. Approximately 500 g of bread is needed.

LOW CARB PERISTOME BREAD

10 mins.
Easy
867 kcal

Ingredients

For 1 Servings

- 60 g wheat bran
- 60 g flaxseed, crushed
- 120 g of oat bran
- 3 eggs)
- 2 tablespoons of water
- 1 teaspoon bread spice mixture
- ½ teaspoon of salt

Nutritional values per serving

- Kcal 867
- Protein 65.62 g
- Fat 48.96 g
- Carbohydrate 41.41 g

Preparation

Approximate working time: 10 minutes
Approximate rest time: 10 minutes
Approximate cooking time: 30 minutes
Approximate total time: 50 minutes

1. Toss all of the ingredients together and soak for 10 minutes. After that, wrap it in a big piece of cling film and roll it up. At the ends, firmly close the transparent video. Wrap it in foil and place it in a pot of boiling water for about 30 minutes.
2. You can, of course, add other herbs or spices to the mix as desired.
3. If you're feeling adventurous, try gluten-free bread.

FIVE MINUTES

normal
1805 kcal

Ingredients

For 1 Portions

- 250 g of dark gluten-free flour
- 150 g of gluten-free light flour
- 100 g of buckwheat flour
- 1 cube of fresh brewer's yeast
- 1 ½ teaspoon of salt
- 430 ml of warm water
- 1 ½ tablespoon of chia seeds
- 2 teaspoons of apple cider vinegar

Nutritional values per serving

- Kcal 1805
- Protein 54.32 g
- Fat 9.76 g
- Carbohydrate 362.67 g

Preparation

Processing time is about 5 minutes.
12 hours of rest is recommended.
1 hour and 10 minutes of cooking/cooking time
The total time is approximately 13 hours and 15 minutes.

1. Heat the water and dissolve the fresh yeast.
2. With a wooden spoon, combine 500 g gluten-free flour, salt, vinegar, chia seeds, and the yeast-water mix (I also use the above mixture) until the flour is no longer visible.
3. Refrigerate the container securely covered for at least 12 hours and up to 5 days, preferably longer.
4. You can cook whenever you want and whenever you have time. Remove the dough from the refrigerator at least 2-3 hours before cooking to allow the

structure to develop.Pour into a greased rectangular mold, cover, and leave in a warm place.

5. Do not preheat the oven—Bake at 200 ° C above and below for about 60 minutes. Remove from the mold and bake for another 10-15 minutes. Take a detonation test.

Tip: This is a flexible recipe with possible variations with bread, spices, cereals, seeds, carrots, and herbs.

JUICY OKARA - FLAX SEEDS – BREAD

10 minutes.
Easy

Ingredients

For 1 Portions

- 1 tablespoon of oil
- 1 teaspoon of vinegar
- 1 sachet of dry yeast
- 50 g of flax seeds
- 450 g of flour
- 150 g of okara
- some soy milk (soy drink), (soy drink)
- 1 teaspoon of salt
- 1 teaspoon of sugar

Preparation

It takes about 10 minutes to complete the processing.
Approximately 10 minutes total

1. The breadmaker places all of the ingredients in the machine and chooses the regular program (about 3 hours). If the batter becomes too dry, add the soy cocktail.
2. The traditional approach is to combine all of the ingredients in a large mixing bowl. The dough is very soft and sticky. Allow 1 hour to rest in a warm position before baking for 55 minutes at 180° C in a preheated oven.
3. It's worth noting that the bread collapses slightly after baking. It has 2,140 calories, 82 grams of protein, 38 grams of fat, and 364 grams of carbohydrates.
4. Okara is a by-product of the manufacture of soy milk or tofu.

SPELLED - BUTTERMILK – BREAD

15 minutes.
Easy
3737 kcal

Ingredients

For 1 Portions

- 500 g of spelled flour
- 500 g of spelled flour
- 2 tablespoons of salt
- 1 teaspoon of sugar
- 1 sachet of yeast
- 850 ml of buttermilk

Nutritional values per serving

- Kcal 3737
- Protein 177.79 g
- Fat 21.94 g
- Carbohydrate 678.22 g

Preparation

Around 15 minutes of processing time
1 hour of standby time
Around 1 hour and 15 minutes total

1. In a cup, combine the yeast and sugar with the hot buttermilk. Sift the two flours into a mixing bowl, make a well in the middle, and stir in the yeast. Mix in a little flour, then gradually add the remaining buttermilk and salt. Knead the dough thoroughly and let it rest for an hour before folding it.
2. Knead the dough once more to shape a loaf of bread. Allow it to cool for 15 minutes before placing it on a greased baking sheet. (Of course, you could use a baking sheet.)
3. Cook for 50 minutes at 220°F.
4. Cereals can be added as well!
5. Delicious and, most importantly, nutritious bread!

CONCLUSION

Many people's diets include bread in various forms, such as toast for breakfast or sandwiches for lunch. It's difficult to keep bread from being hard and moldy in less than a week, a process known as staleness. In certain countries, the type of bread baked must be consumed within a few hours of being baked (for example, baguettes). Small bakeries are still a significant shop in some countries because they are difficult to maintain. Bread does not hold well in the refrigerator, but it can be frozen, so buy a loaf, split it in half, and freeze one half. Enjoy!